SEASONAL GUIDE
TO THE NATURAL YEAR

Northern
California

SEASONAL
GUIDE
TO THE
NATURAL
YEAR

Bill McMillon

A Month by Month Guide to Natural Events

FULCRUM PUBLISHING
Golden, Colorado

McMillon, Bill.
    Seasonal guide to the natural year : a month by month guide to natural events.   Northern California / by Bill McMillon.
        p.   cm.
    Includes bibliographical references (p.) and index.
    ISBN 1-55591-157-9
    1. Natural history—California, Northern—Guidebooks.
    2. California, Northern—Guidebooks.   3 Seasons—California,
    Northern.   I. Title.
    QH105.C2M36   1995
    508.794—dc20   94-37286
                                                                             CIP

Book design and cover illustrations by Paulette Livers Lambert
Photographs by Bill McMillon

Maps included in this book are for general reference only. For more detailed maps and additional information, contact the agencies or specific sites listed in the appendix.

Printed in the United States of America

0   9   8   7   6   5   4   3   2

Fulcrum Publishing
350 Indiana Street, Suite 350
Golden, Colorado 80401-5093
(800) 992-2908

CONTENTS

LIST OF MAPS

INTRODUCTION

California has no seasons, at least according to many Easterners who are used to four definite seasons easily identified by the changes in the weather, brilliant fall foliage and heavy winter snowfall. For those of us who live in California and spend a lot of time in nature that idea is absurd. There are very definite seasonal changes in Northern California. They are just more subtle than those found east of the 100th parallel, and it takes a while to get used to them. I know it took me several years after I moved to California from rural Mississippi in the 1950s.

A normal seasonal pattern in nature is migration— whether the annual trek of gray whales from the Arctic Ocean to the calving lagoons along the coast of Baja California and back again or of California newts from one pond to another in Briones Regional Park near San Francisco—and occasionally there are even human migrations. In the past hundred years one has occurred in America that dramatically changed the way Americans related to nature and seasonal changes. This was the migration of large numbers of people from farms and small towns to heavily populated urban areas.

People who live in rural areas, particularly those such as farmers who work in the outdoors, are more in tune with the rhythms of seasonal changes than those who live in cities. Most who live in large urban centers have no need to be aware of the constant changes that occur in nature as the year progresses and frequently lose contact with natural events that occur seasonally. Alarm clocks, electric lights, central heating and air conditioning act as buffers between people and seasonal changes in nature, and looking at the changing pages of a calendar is no substitute for observing the changing colors on the trees outside.

My family was a part of the migration from farm to city in the 1950s, and it took me time to realize how our move from a farm in Mississippi to a large city in California affected my relationship with nature. As a child I often stopped work in the fields in late autumn to watch a V formation of migrating geese pass overhead along the Mississippi Flyway. Later, as a teen, I watched similar gaggles pass over my home along the Pacific Flyway in the Great Central Valley of California. I was always fascinated by these seasonal flights, but in retrospect realize those of my early years had much more meaning to me.

At that time my life revolved around the seasons much as did the lives of the vast flights of geese migrating to their winter feeding sites from their summer homes in the Arctic north. As a farm family we followed the seasons as closely as any wild animals. Spring was the time we tilled the soil and planted our crops. Early summer was a busy period as we tended young seedlings while they sprouted and grew toward maturity. Midsummer was a period of relaxation and repair as we waited for the busy harvest period of autumn. Winter was when we slaughtered hogs for our yearly meat supply, shelled corn for the livestock and brought in cords of wood to ward off the chill of the cold, wet winds that penetrated the barrier of newspapers and cardboard covering the open cracks in the walls of our house.

It was impossible for us to ignore the changing seasons or to be unaware of the natural events that accompanied each change. That wasn't so after we moved to the city, where life's rhythms were controlled more by clocks and calendars than by natural events. Modern conveniences made sunrise and sunset or the cold of winter and heat of summer irrelevant. We could, and generally did, ignore what went on in nature. We only observed or participated in seasonal changes when we wanted, and that was a shame. We lost our most elemental contact with the natural world, and I missed it immensely.

In my late teens I began to search for this lost contact, and found that I had little knowledge of what really went on in my new world. I could still tell you what happened in nature each month at my old home but had little feel for the monthly changes in my new one. And one excuse was that California really didn't have the seasonal changes that the lands east of the Mississippi did.

The myth, and one I readily accepted at the time, was that there were only two seasons in California. Summer, which was hot and dry, and winter, which was wet and cold. It took me a number of years to recognize the myth for what it was, and today I enjoy changes such as the emerald green growth on hillsides during late winter and early spring and the exuberant blue and gold colors of poppies and lupine that later pop out of the green carpet.

I now know these brilliant displays of color will give way to hills of golden brown by midsummer and then turn to a washed-out gray as the winter rains begin the process all over again.

Each of these is accompanied by many other seasonal changes in the flora and fauna of Northern California, from the geese and ducks that come south to winter at the wildlife refuges set aside in the remaining wetlands of the Central Valley to the eruption of mushrooms and fungi in the redwood forests along the coast and the riparian woodlands of the Central Valley after the first fall rains.

I now also know that on a trip from the coast inland to the ridges of the Sierra Nevada I encounter as many life zones as I would if I traveled from Mexico to the Canadian arctic.

A good sampling of the seasonal events of Northern California is described in this guide, which is one with a difference. Instead of just listing *where* natural sites are in Northern California it lists *when* natural events occur at various sites. Of course it tells you how to get to the sites to see these seasonal events, but the emphasis is on timing, not geography.

Built on a seasonal theme, the book is divided into twelve monthly sections, each with at least four wild events of unusual interest. "Hotspots" where these events can be easily observed are listed, and directions and tips on how to best enjoy the outings are provided for each event, as well as some natural history of the sites.

Each section also includes an in-depth look at an unusual or "Breakout" event that occurs that month.

The book covers a broad expanse of California from the Oregon border in the north to a loosely drawn boundary that extends from the southern end of Monterey County on the west to Bishop on the east. This region is one of great diversity, and amateur naturalists are never at a loss to find interesting events to observe at any time of the year.

Although this region is only part of one state, it is still vast, covering some 75,000 square miles, and is one of the most geologically and ecologically diverse region of its size in the United States. Mt. Whitney, the highest point in the contiguous United States at 14,404 feet, is found here, as is the huge (300 miles long and 50 miles wide), flat Central Valley that is the drainage of both the Sacramento and San Joaquin river systems. The high peaks of the Sierra Nevada with their huge outcroppings of granite give way to the more recent, and lower, volcanic peaks of the Cascade Mountains to the north, and they in turn merge with the high, lava-covered Modoc plateau. These vast, sparsely populated areas lie along the eastern border of the state.

To the west of the Central Valley are the much lower, but still rugged, mountains of the Coast Range, which stretches almost a thousand miles from Oregon to Mexico. The coastal redwoods grow in the northern tier of this range, and their forests are home to much flora and fauna that are found nowhere else in the state.

The Sacramento/San Joaquin Delta and the San Francisco Bay regions include important wetlands and estuaries where wildlife congregates, and the Monterey Bay area is home to exciting congregations of birds.

All in all the region is a rich land that is a naturalist's dream, and there is an abundance of sites where access is easy and unfettered. In the San Francisco Bay area alone there are 125 state, county and national parks, a largely undeveloped coastline, canyons with tall forests of redwoods, mountain slopes covered with dense chaparral and almost fifty lakes. These numbers become even more impressive as you leave the Bay area. With large national parks such as Lassen and Yosemite, dozens of state parks, two of the largest national wildlife complexes in the country and millions of acres of national forest (there are over 18 million acres of national forest in the whole state), naturalists enjoy easy access to a wide variety of natural events year round in Northern California.

GENERAL TIPS, CAUTIONS AND SUGGESTIONS

Almost all of the places in this guide are on public lands, or on lands administered by land trusts such as The Nature Conservancy. This does not mean that the sites should be treated with any less respect than you would give privately owned land, though, and visitors should always be aware of any special rules and regulations that are in effect at a particular site.

These rules are seldom, if ever, arbitrarily imposed, and they protect the very spectacles that visitors come to see. If nesting birds are disturbed during crucial periods the yearly hatch may be threatened. If the territory of rutting elk is invaded the herd may be harmed, not to mention the damage that might come to those who invade the territory.

The wild animals and plants described in the book are not here just to be celebrated by humans. They exist quite separately from us and seldom benefit from human intervention. To insure that our observations bring about minimal destruction, please stay on marked trails and obey all signs restricting access to a particular area or refuge.

Remember, those who cause the least effect on the natural events they are watching are the best observers.

Although the book includes thorough directions to all of the sites, you should always have several detailed maps of the areas you intend to visit. State highway and travel club maps are fine for sites that are near major routes, but those located on backroads are unlikely to be covered. There are several options that are much better.

For general information on back roads the *Northern California Atlas & Gazetteer* published by the DeLorme Mapping Company is an excellent source. You will also need the Southern California edition for some of the sites along the southern part of the region. I use this atlas extensively on my travels around the state and have never found it lacking. Occasionally I need more specific maps of a region, however, and then utilize two types of government publications.

The U.S. Forest Service (USFS) produces maps of all national forest land in California, and these highlight the many dirt logging roads maintained by the USFS. I find these useful when I am in unfamiliar country and may need to stray from well-maintained roads to reach a site. They tend to be the most up-to-date maps of the roads in national forests and also show many natural sites that the USFS deems interesting or important.

If I am going to leave my vehicle and head into backcountry to a site, I make sure that I have a U.S. Geological Survey (USGS) topographical map of the area. These maps only cover small areas (the 7.5-minute quadrangles cover an area of about 6.5 by 7.5 miles) and are too bulky to use in the car as road maps. They are absolutely essential, however, when you need to know the topography of an area where you are hiking.

Be aware that many of the trails on these maps may not be current, so check with someone who knows the area if you don't want to end up bushwhacking crosscountry to reach your destination.

Getting lost is only one safety factor you should be concerned with. Many of the sites in the book are on land where hunters roam freely during season—during autumn and winter be sure to check about hunting in the area before you leave for the field. If it is hunting season, wear a bright orange cap and/or vest to let hunters know you are there.

While some readers may feel hunting should not be allowed, or not allowed in special refuges, remember that almost all state game or wildlife management land, as well as much national wildlife refuge land, was purchased by fishing and hunting license fees and would not be protected from development without those funds.

Some of the sites in the book are best viewed by canoe. If you choose to use a canoe, learn the basics of canoe handling before you set out on the trip and be sure to wear flotation devices even if you are a strong swimmer.

Finally, be sure to dress for the weather. Northern California is noted for the diversity of its weather as much as for any other natural diversity, and on some outings you will be faced with changing weather that will require you to be prepared for everything from sun and heat to fog and cold. If you do not know the weather patterns of the region where you are headed, find out before you leave. Hypothermia or heat prostration are no fun.

A REQUEST FOR HELP

I have made every attempt to give accurate, up-to-date directions to the sites in the book, but things change over time. Roads are rerouted, bridges wash out and major landmarks may be torn down. If readers find that my directions are inaccurate or insufficient please let us know. Readers are encouraged to send current, accurate information about a site to the author, c/o Fulcrum Publishing, 350 Indiana Street, Suite 350, Golden, CO 80401.

The diversity of Northern California is great, and the number of natural events included in this book are necessarily limited. If I have left out events you think should be included in future editions please send them to the above address (with directions and as much background as possible). Remember that the events should be consistent in time and place from year to year, they should be exceptional or unusual and they should occur on public land or private land that is open to the public.

Abbreviations commonly used in the text:

NP	National Park
NWR	National Wildlife Refuge
SP	State Park
SRA	State Recreation Area

JANUARY

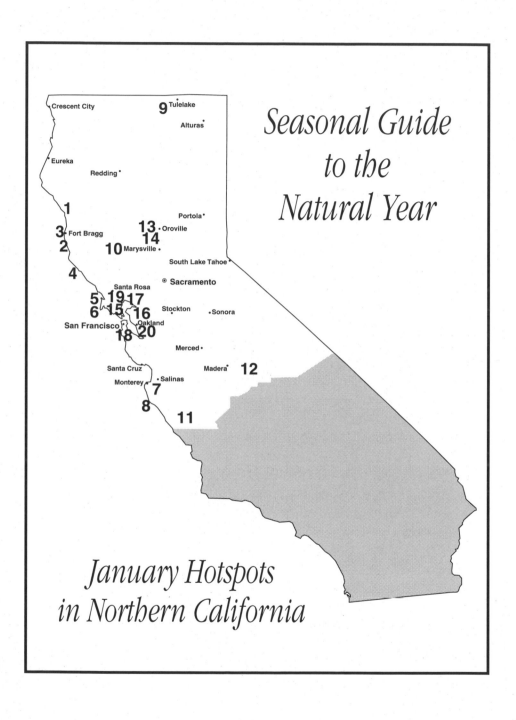

Crescent City

9 Tulelake

Alturas

Eureka

Redding

1

Portola

13 Oroville

3 Fort Bragg

14

2

10 Marysville

South Lake Tahoe

4

⊚ Sacramento

Santa Rosa

5 19 17

6 15 16

Stockton

Sonora

San Francisco

Oakland

18 20

Merced

Madera

12

Santa Cruz

Salinas

Monterey

7

8

11

*Seasonal Guide
to the
Natural Year*

*January Hotspots
in Northern California*

MAP SITE KEY

1. McKerricher SP
2. Mendocino Headlands SP
3. Manchester Beach SP
4. Salt Point SP
5. Bodega Head
6. Point Reyes National Seashore
7. Point Lobos State Reserve
8. Andrew Molera SP
9. Klamath Basin NWR Complex
10. Cache Creek Canyon
11. Lake San Antonio County Park
12. Millerton Lake SRA
13. Sacramento NWR Complex
14. Gray Lodge Wildlife Area
15. Mount Tamalpais
16. Mount Diablo
17. Mount Livermore
18. San Bruno Mountain
19. Mount St. Helena
20. Tilden Regional Park

January Observations

1

Migrating Gray Whales

The gray whale is a magnificent creature that can reach 45 feet in length and weigh 45 tons at maturity, but even this size did not keep the species from being ravaged by whalers in the nineteenth century. By 1900, only about two thousand gray whales survived in the world's oceans, and their numbers continued to decrease until commercial hunting of them was banned in 1939.

Although they are still threatened by industrial development near their calving lagoons along the coast of Baja California and oil development throughout their range, the grays have made a remarkable comeback since hunting was banned. Their population now exceeds twenty-one thousand (which some authorities believe approaches their prehistoric levels), and almost all of these follow an annual 6,000-mile route from their feeding grounds in the Bering Sea to lagoons along the Pacific Coast of Baja California where pregnant females give birth and then mate before returning north.

All of the whales fast during the six months they take to make the round trip, but gorge themselves on various amphipods (small shrimplike creatures) at their feeding grounds off the coast of Alaska during the summer.

The gray whale was removed from the endangered species list in early 1994, the first marine mammal ever removed from the list, and it is flourishing. And with their habit of traveling relatively close to the shore on their migration, a whole new industry, whale-watching, is also flourishing. Unlike the whaling industry of the nineteenth century, however, the new one is not dangerous to the whales.

Naturalists estimate that 94 percent of the population that feeds in the Bering Sea during the summer passes within a mile of Point Reyes in Marin County between December and February. Most of these pass during the first two weeks in January when as many as two thousand whales go by in a day. The whales' annual trek has been joined by a trek of humans to the coast to catch a glimpse of the giants rising to the surface to spout their telltale spray. Occasionally observers see a glistening, barnacle-covered back as a whale rises out of the water, or a large set of flukes as it dives below the surface.

While the whales pass closest to shore at Point Reyes, it is only one of a number of excellent whale-watching sites along the coast of Northern California that stretch from near the Oregon border to Monterey County. In addition, many party boats take time out from fishing to carry interested observers out to sea where they encounter the grays up close.

Pregnant females lead the parade south, since they want to get to warm waters where their 12-foot-long infants can survive more easily. They are followed by nonpregnant females, then older males and finally adolescent males, who bring up the rear. The young males are sometimes so far behind that they never reach the warm waters of Mexico. As they are met by the first of the older whales returning north for food they turn and lead the trek back to the Bering Sea. The rest of the order of migrating whales is also reversed, with the mothers with calves bringing up the rear.

Seagulls flock to feeding areas on winter beaches.

The herds of whales are farther from shore on the return trip, which takes place around the end of March, but serious whale-watchers still search for them from the tall bluffs.

HOTSPOTS

Just about any point of land that extends into the Pacific off the coast of California and has high bluffs is a hotspot, but several stand out as superior to others. California Highway 1 follows the coast from above **Fort Bragg** to **Big Sur**, and most of the best sites to spot gray whales are found along this route. These are all easily accessible, and anyone can enjoy watching for the spouts of the whales as they surface to refill their lungs with fresh air.

Several words of warning. Winters along the coast can be cold. While the temperatures may be mild, the damp winds that come off the ocean can make even moderate temperatures seem frigid. Winter waves can also be dangerous. Storms that form in the northern Pacific often have high winds that push huge waves ashore along the coast. Occasionally a rogue wave much larger than all the others will crash ashore, and even reach to the tops of the high bluffs that whale-watchers prefer. Keep an eye out for these, for people have been washed out to sea from the bluffs, particularly from Mendocino County north.

With these warnings in mind, enjoy your whale-watching expedition. Wear warm clothes that will keep you dry and bring binoculars, cameras with telephoto lenses or telescopes on tripods to get the best views of the whales.

Seasoned whale-watchers each have their favorite spots, but most people head for the **coastal bluffs of Mendocino County**; **Salt Point SP** and **Bodega Head** in Sonoma County; **Point Reyes Lighthouse** in **Point Reyes National Seashore** or **Point Lobos State Reserve** and **Andrew Molera SP** in Monterey County.

There are three sites along the **Mendocino Coast** where whale-watching is excellent. The first is **McKerricher SP**, which is located several miles north of Fort Bragg on California Highway 1. The migrating herds come in close to the shore as they pass **Laguna Point** in this park. The entrance to the park is on CA 1 north of Fort Bragg. Ask for directions to Point Laguna at the ranger station.

Farther south is one of the most popular viewing sites along the entire California coast. The **Mendocino Headlands SP** is the whale-watching center of the Mendocino coast, for the peninsula where the park is located juts far out into the Pacific. Whale-watchers have outstanding views as the whales come close as they round the bluffs of the headlands.

There is plenty of general information about whale-watching along the coast at the Ford House visitors' center at the park, which lies along CA 1 south of the picturesque village of Mendocino.

About 30 miles south of Mendocino and a mile north of the small community of Point Arena is another of the outstanding sites for whale-watching in Mendocino County. **Manchester Beach SP** also sits on a point that juts into the

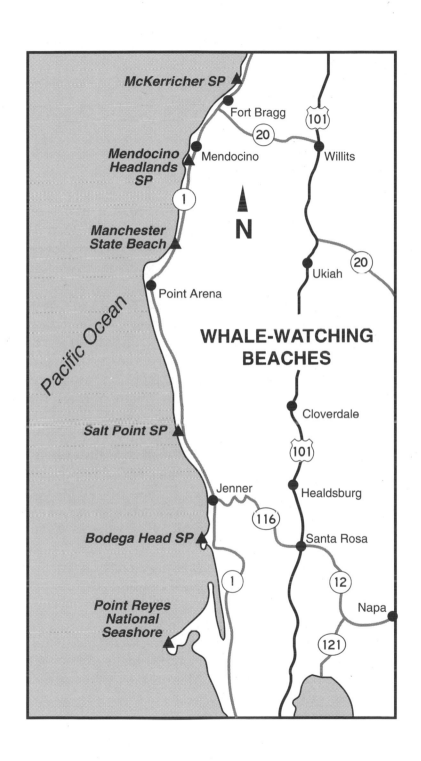

McKerricher SP

Fort Bragg

101

20

Mendocino
Headlands
SP

Mendocino

Willits

1

Manchester
State Beach

N

Point Arena

20

Ukiah

**WHALE-WATCHING
BEACHES**

Cloverdale

Salt Point SP

101

Jenner

Healdsburg

116

Bodega Head SP

Santa Rosa

1

12

Point Reyes
National
Seashore

Napa

121

Pacific Ocean

Pacific, and whale-watching from its high bluffs is excellent. Follow the signs from CA 1 to the park.

In Sonoma County whale-watchers gather at either **Salt Point SP**, which is located along CA 1 about 15 miles north of Jenner, or at **Bodega Head**, about 15 miles south of Jenner. From Jenner, where CA 116 ends at CA 1 near the mouth of the Russian River, follow the signs along CA 1 to Salt Point SP. Ask at the ranger station where the best whale-watching is in the park.

To reach Bodega Head take Bay Flat Road off CA 1 in the small town of Bodega Bay south of Jenner and continue for just under 4 miles until it dead-ends at a parking lot on the bluffs of the head. You will pass by a large hole in the ground, now filled with water, on the way to the bluffs that was the proposed site of a nuclear power plant in the 1950s. The site was abandoned after a public outcry about building such a plant above the very active San Andreas Fault, which runs directly beneath the head.

Probably the most popular site for whale-watching is the old lighthouse that stands on the bluffs near **Drakes Beach** in the **Point Reyes National Seashore**. This site is unsurpassed for its setting, and the herds come very close to shore at this point. You can reach the seashore by taking Sir Francis Drake Boulevard off CA 1 just south of Point Reyes Station and continuing for about 15 miles to the lighthouse. During the migrating season there is generally a ranger at the lighthouse parking lot to provide information to whale-watchers.

Farther south, along the central coast of California, enjoy whale-watching at **Point Lobos State Reserve**, which is off CA 1 several miles south of Carmel. This is where the endangered California sea otter finds sanctuary, as well as at **Andrew Molera SP**, 22 miles south of Carmel on CA 1.

At Point Lobos ask at the ranger station which coves you can best see the whales in. The road in the park follows the coastline south for about 3 miles, and there are several spots where you may see spouts.

The best spot to see whales at Andrew Molera SP, the largest state park in the Big Sur area, entails about a 1-mile hike along the **Headlands Trail** to **Molera Point**.

In Monterey itself you can often see gray whales in Monterey Bay, and the Monterey Bay Aquarium provides telescopes and naturalists on its outdoor, oceanfront decks.

For those who wish to get a closer look at these marine behemoths, a number of organizations offer naturalist-led boat trips to spots off the coast where the whales are likely to surface. In **Noyo Harbor** near Fort Bragg and the harbor at **Bodega Bay** party fishing boats frequently take whale-watching groups out. For more information on these call the Mendocino Coast Chamber of Commerce at (800) 726-2780 or the Bodega Bay Area Chamber of Commerce at (707) 875-3422.

The Oceanic Society Expeditions and the Whale Center both lead trips from **Half Moon Bay** and **San Francisco**. You can reach The Oceanic Society, a nonprofit environmental education group, at (415) 474-3385, for more information about their trips. The Whale Center, which is also a nonprofit educational group, can be reached at (510) 654-6621.

The Monterey Bay Aquarium also leads whale-watching trips from the **Monterey Harbor**. They can be reached at (408) 648-4926.

Finally, the towns of Mendocino and Fort Bragg have Whale Festivals around the first weekend of March each year at the end of the migration. You can call the Mendocino Coast Chamber of Commerce at the above number for more information on these.

2

Wintering Bald Eagles

The bald eagle is said to be one large fieldmark as it soars against the winter sky. The white head and tail of mature bald eagles are unlike any other bird in America, and this striking bird has caught the fancy of Americans since the early Europeans settled our country. The majesty of this raptor led it to be named our national bird, but its feeding habits almost led to its demise in the 1940s, 1950s and 1960s.

Bald eagles feed primarily on fish and carrion, and the pesticide DDT became concentrated in fish between 1940 and 1960. As with other raptors such as the peregrine falcon, bald eagles' eggs became thin and easily broken as the adult birds' systems were contaminated with the pesticide. This brought about a rapid decline in the eagle population all across the nation, and they were placed on the endangered animal list.

DDT was banned in 1972, but it has taken years to flush it out of the ecosystem. During that time it was a treat to spot a single bald eagle, much less the more typical flocks that historically congregated near a feeding place where food was readily available, around the wetlands and lakes of Northern California. Today, however, the bald eagle has almost returned to its former numbers, and there is talk of removing it from the endangered list.

Nowhere is this more evident than at several Northern California locations. In fact, one of the largest gatherings of bald eagles in the lower forty-eight states is found in the Klamath Basin in the northeast corner of the state near the Oregon border. Several large national wildlife refuges, all part of the Klamath NWR Complex, are located within the region. These include lakes and wetlands where vast numbers of waterfowl winter or stop on their way farther south.

During the freezes that occur each winter in the region, many of the waterfowl, including the large Canada geese, die of hunger and exposure. These, along with the fish that live in the lakes, provide easy food for a group of some five hundred bald eagles that migrate south each winter from Canada and Alaska.

These roost in tall trees in the Bear Valley NWR outside of Worden, Oregon, and fly out each morning to feed at the Tule Lake and Lower Klamath refuges across the border in California.

At first glance the flock seems to be a mixture of bald and golden eagles. Many of the birds are almost completely brown and lack the telltale white heads and tails that are the field identification marks of the bald eagle. The brown birds are not golden eagles, as many people think, but immature bald eagles that will not gain their very noticeable white heads and tails until they are five years old.

During their first year out of the nest young bald eagles are completely brown except for a small strip of white under their wings and a white marking under their armpits. After their second-year molt the young eagles retain their brown heads and chests, but have plenty of white on their underbellies. The first white on the tails of the immature eagles also appears at this time. The brown tail feathers of the first year are replaced with white feathers that have a wide brown band, much like the tail markings of young golden eagles.

By the third year more and more white feathers grow out after the molt, and the adolescent bald eagles have heavily-streaked chests and upper bodies. The white patches on the underside of their wings have also become much larger.

The young bald eagles begin to look more like adults during their fourth year. The molt during this year is a long, drawn-out process during which the birds are rather seedy looking. An uneven combination of brown, gray and white markings can be seen all over the bird. The head has yet to attain its pure white feathers, and it requires a good view to determine that the white feathers are emerging.

You will see birds at all these stages of maturity in the flock, and I like to try to count how many of each stage are included in a flock as it flies over.

At any bald eagle congregation point there are other large birds that feed on carrion, and many people confuse them with the eagles. These are turkey vultures, but you can differentiate them from eagles by their flight patterns. Eagles soar with their wings held almost flat, and their heads extend far forward from the wings. Vultures soar with their wings held in a distinctive V shape, and their heads are tiny in comparison to those of eagles.

HOTSPOTS

There are four major spots to sight wintering bald eagles in Northern California. These are the Klamath Basin region, Cache Creek in Lake County, Lake San Antonio in Monterey County, and Millerton Lake near Fresno.

The **Klamath Basin** area has the largest congregation of eagles, and they are readily seen by car about two hours after sunrise. From Klamath Falls, Oregon, drive 11 miles south to Worden. Take U.S. 97 south out of Worden for 3/4 mile, and turn right at the sign to Keno. As you cross the railroad tracks go left and continue about 1 mile. Park along the road and look to the northwest. The eagles fly out of the trees toward the refuges to the south.

An auto tour of the **Lower Klamath NWR** takes you through some prime viewing areas where the eagles feed. Both a CALTRANS (California Department of Transportation) vista point and the beginning of an auto tour are located 9 miles east of U.S. 97 on CA 161. CA 161 is about 25 miles south of Klamath Falls. The information plaques at the vista point give you information about the auto tour.

If you want information about other viewing opportunities in the refuge you can visit the refuge headquarters and visitors' center by continuing east on CA 161 8 miles to Hill Road. Turn south and go 4 miles to the visitors' center. You can call or write the headquarters beforehand for information at Klamath Basin National Wildlife Complex, Route 1, Box 74, Tulelake, CA 96134; (916) 667-2231.

For a more strenuous outing you can hike into **Cache Creek Canyon** in Lake County about 60 miles north of San Francisco. The U.S. Bureau of Land Management and the California Department of Fish and Game have combined efforts to protect two endangered species that live inside the **Cache Creek Wilderness Study Area**, which is planned to become the largest oak woodland wilderness preserve in California. One is the bald eagle, and the other is the tule elk. More than fifty bald eagles winter in the tall trees above Cache Creek as a four hundred-strong herd of tule elk browse on the hillsides below.

The 7-mile long **Redbud Trail** begins on the south side of CA 20 just west of the North Fork of Cache Creek. You reach the trailhead by following CA 20 33 miles west from its intersection with I-5 at Williams. Trail maps are available at the trailhead.

There are viewing sites at **Baton Flat**, about 2 miles from the trailhead, and at **Wilson Valley**, about 6 miles in. The largest concentration of eagles is found in Wilson Valley, however.

There is some indication that there is at least one breeding pair of bald eagles in the area, although this has not been confirmed.

For more information about this site contact the Bureau of Land Management, Clear Lake Resource Area, 555 Leslie St., Ukiah, CA 95482; (707) 462-3873.

More leisurely viewings of bald eagles are found at **Lake San Antonio County Park**, near King City in Monterey County and **Millerton Lake SRA** near Fresno. Boat tours led by park naturalists are offered at both of these locations each January through March to view golden and bald eagle habitats. For information about the Lake San Antonio tours call (408) 755-4899. For Millerton Lake call (209) 822-2710.

You reach Lake San Antonio by the Lake Nacimiento exit off U.S. 101 in Paso Robles. Turn left on CA 46/G-14 and follow it for 26 miles to San Antonio Road. Turn right on San Antonio Road and continue to the lake.

You reach Millerton Lake off CA 99. Take the Madera exit to CA 145. Follow CA 145 22 miles to the lake.

3

Gaggles of Canada Geese

The mountains to the west of the Sacramento NWR form a dark silhouette against late evening skies, and the light from the sinking sun often tints the sky and thin wisps of clouds above a slowly darkening pink. Long shadows from the mountains reflect in ponds where thousands of ducks and geese have difficulty settling in for the night. Without warning, a flock will rise from one pond, the pink light highlighting their flapping wings, only to land in another a short distance away. Each landing is accompanied by loud cackling as fowl fight for a place on the water.

This visual experience is enjoyed by thousands of visitors to the several state and national wildlife refuges of the upper Sacramento Valley each winter, as hundreds of thousands of waterfowl use the Pacific Flyway on their migration south from their summer homes in Alaska and Canada to winter feeding grounds in the Sacramento Valley. Although these are impressive flocks as they move from one feeding site to another, they are minuscule in comparison to the ones observed by the early Europeans who settled California.

In the nineteenth century rivers regularly flooded their banks and spread over many thousands of acres of the valley floor, creating vast wetlands where millions of water-fowl spent the winter. The concentration of ducks and geese was so thick they were said to blacken the sky as the huge flocks moved from one feeding site to another. Today, more than 95 percent of the wetlands that were scattered over the valley floor in the nineteenth century have been destroyed, and that has taken a toll on the waterfowl population.

Less than 300,000 acres are now in public and private refuges and preserves, but these are the winter feeding grounds for up to one million migrating waterfowl each year. Nowhere else in North America are so many waterfowl so dependent upon so few acres of wetlands. This concentration of fowl does have one benefit, however, for it makes it easy to observe large flocks of fowl in a small area.

The endangered Aleutian Canada goose winters exclusively in the Central Valley, and the region is the primary wintering area of the cackling Canada goose, lesser snow goose, Ross's goose, tule white-fronted goose, snow goose and the northern pintail duck. Combined, these species form impressive flocks that can be seen rising from refuge feeding ponds at dawn and dusk every day.

The flocks of Canada geese, one of the largest and most colorful of the migrating waterfowl, reach their greatest numbers in January, which is the best time to visit the refuges that are located between I-5 and the Sacramento River in the upper Sacramento Valley.

HOTSPOTS

The easiest of the refuges to reach is the **Sacramento NWR Complex**. Traveling north on I-5 take the Norman Road Exit 18 miles north of Williams and head north on the frontage road for about 1.5 miles to the refuge entrance.

A 6-mile long, self-guided auto tour follows dirt roads on top of levees through the refuge, and a self-guiding walking tour begins at the visitors' center. Both are open sunrise to sunset year round. The visitors' center hours vary by season.

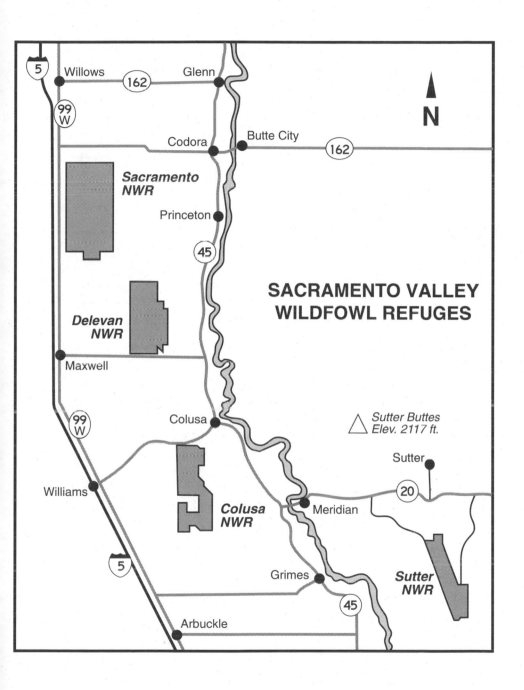

N

Willows 5 162 Glenn

99 W

Codora Butte City 162

Sacramento NWR

Princeton 45

SACRAMENTO VALLEY
WILDFOWL REFUGES

Delevan NWR

Maxwell

99 W

Colusa

Sutter Buttes
Elev. 2117 ft.

Sutter

Williams

Colusa NWR

Meridian 20

5

Grimes 45

Sutter NWR

Arbuckle

For recorded information about waterfowl population, visitors' center hours and public use information call (916) 934-7774. This number also provides information about the other national wildlife refuges (Colusa, Delevan, and Sutter) that are part of the complex. Call (916) 934-2801 to contact the refuge personally.

The entrance to the **Colusa NWR** is located .5 mile west of the small town of Colusa on CA 20. For **Delevan NWR** take Maxwell Road off I-5 about 9 miles north of Williams and continue east to Four Mile Road. This road runs along the western boundary of the refuge, which has no public access. **Sutter NWR** is somewhat more difficult to reach. From Yuba City, which is located north of Sacramento on CA 99, take CA 20 west to George Washington Boulevard, where you turn south on Oswald Road. Turn west on Hughes Road, which bisects the refuge.

The California Department of Fish and Game also operates several wildlife refuges in the region, and the best of these for observing the wintering waterfowl is the **Gray Lodge Wildlife Area**. This 6,600-acre preserve is located just north of the Sutter Buttes (often called the smallest mountain range in the world) in the Butte Sink region. In addition to the vast numbers of waterfowl, sandhill cranes winter here in large numbers. To reach Gray Lodge take CA 99 north from Yuba City for 10 miles to Live Oak. Turn west on Pennington Road (also called North Butte) in Live Oak to Almond Orchard Road. Turn north and continue to refuge entrance. The refuge is about 8 miles from Live Oak.

4

Climbing Peaks of the San Francisco Bay Area

Once upon a time before modern civilization and its air pollution intruded upon the pristine wilderness of Northern California, you could see almost forever from the peaks that rise above the San Francisco Bay area. In fact, the view from one—Mt. Diablo—was said to be second only to Mt. Kilamanjaro for the amount of land that can be seen from one peak.

On a clear winter's day in the last century one could see to Mt. Shasta to the north, all of the Sierra Nevada peaks as far south as Yosemite and west for over 50 miles to the Farallon Islands some 26 miles off the Golden Gate. This panoramic view included all of the northern section the Central Valley, and such highlights as the Sutter Buttes that rise from the valley floor north of Yuba City, the waterways of the Sacramento/San Joaquin Delta and a broad expanse of the lower valley.

Today's air quality—although better than it was a decade ago—does not provide such clarity, but on clear winter days after a storm has passed through and an inversion layer has not formed to trap haze and pollutants over the valley, you can see the snow-covered Sierra peaks as they stand in sharp contrast against the blue sky, as well as Mt. Lassen to the north. On an exceptional day you may see Mt. Shasta through the haze far to the north.

Mt. Diablo is only one of a number of peaks in the region that offer breathtaking vistas that are well worth the effort required to reach the top. Some, such as Mt. Diablo and Mt. Tamalpais, have roads that lead almost to the peak, while others, such as Mt. St. Helena, can only be reached after a strenuous hike.

To enjoy the best views, wait until a large storm has passed through, maybe one that drops a light blanket of snow on the higher peaks in the region on its way to the Sierra Nevada where a much heavier blanket covers the slopes. Get an early start so you reach the peak by midmorning, and you will be delighted with the sparkle that highlights the distant views.

HOTSPOTS

Mt. Diablo, at 3,849 feet, is the centerpiece of **Mt. Diablo SP**, and is located about 20 miles east of Oakland in Contra Costa County. You get to the summit by taking Ygnacio Valley Road east off I-680 in Walnut Creek. At North Gate Road turn south and continue until you reach the parking lot at the summit. There is a level, .5-mile trail that circles the peak, and there is an observation deck on top.

Mt. Tamalpais is an easy drive north of the Golden Gate Bridge in Marin County. This 2,571-foot peak is lower than Mt. Diablo and does not offer quite the view. The view of downtown San Francisco, the Golden Gate and San Francisco/Oakland Bay bridges, the cities of the East Bay and the rolling hills of Sonoma County to the north are nevertheless spectacular. Take the Stinson Beach exit off U.S. 101 just past Sausalito. Stay on CA 1 for about 3 miles and then turn right on the Panoramic Highway. Follow Panoramic Highway as it takes a circuitous route up the slopes of Mt. Tamalpais until you reach Southside Road. Turn right on Southside Road and continue 1 mile to

Ridgecrest Boulevard. Turn right on Ridgecrest and go 3 miles to the parking lot at the summit. The 1.5-mile **Verna Dunshee Trail** circles the summit, and a .5 mile side trail leads to the lookout tower on top.

Mt. Livermore is the highest point on Angel Island at 781 feet, and the 3.5-mile **Sunset/North Ridge Trails** loop offers a moderate outing for those who wish a bird's eye view of San Francisco and the inner bay. **Angel Island SP** is served by ferries from San Francisco ((415) 546-2896) and Tiburon ((415) 435-2131). Pick up a map of the island at the visitors' center near the ferry terminal.

San Bruno Mountain is located south of San Francisco in the **San Bruno Mountain State and County Park**. The hike to the top of San Bruno Mountain is a strenuous 6-mile loop, but the view of the peninsula to the south, San Francisco to the north and the hills of the East Bay are well worth the effort. Those who want most of the views with less effort can take the **Saddle/Bog Trails** loop on the north side of the park. This trail has an outstanding view of downtown San Francisco as it looks right down Market Street to the San Francisco/Oakland Bay Bridge. Take Guadalupe Canyon Parkway west from U.S. 101 to the park. Follow the signs to the parking lots. Park in the south lot for the climb to the top of the peak, and the north lot for the Saddle/Bog Trails loop.

Mt. St. Helena is the highest peak in the San Francisco Bay region at 4,343 feet and one of the most difficult to reach. From the parking lot for the **Robert Louis Stevenson SP** on CA 29 north of Calistoga you must take a 5-mile trail to the peak. After the first mile this hike follows an open fire road as it winds around the mountain. On cool winter mornings the bright sun feels good as it takes the edge off the morning chill. Be sure to wear warm, layered clothes since the peak may be very cold in the winter, but it is often warmer at the top of the peak than the beginning of the trail.

5

January Shorttakes

BIRD FEEDERS

This is the time to fill your bird feeders and watch the winter habitants of the region come to your windows. Count how many different species you attract and change your feed to attract different birds. The Audubon Society has a feeder watch program that you can participate in.

FOG WALKS ALONG RIPARIAN TRAILS

The combination of cold nights and wet ground makes for thick pockets of fog in wet areas, and I enjoy walking along creeks and around lakes and ponds when the fog is just burning off as the morning sun pushes its way through the fog.

OREGON JUNCOS

This small bird migrates in large flocks to winter over in Northern California. This is a good time to watch these flocks, either at home feeders or in parks where they flit around searching for food. You can tell the most recent arrivals for they are much skinnier than those that have had time to fatten up.

6

Breakout: Mating Newts

The answer to the question of "Why did the male newt cross the road?" is easy, according to David Zuckerman, a naturalist with the East Bay Regional Parks District. It's to get from the wooded hills of Tilden Regional Park in the Berkeley Hills where they hibernate between April and October to the moss-covered banks of Wildcat Creek. There he will turn from a slim land dweller into a bloated water lover ready for a mate.

The males make this trip about a month ahead of the females, but both have a difficult time surviving a 15-minute crossing of South Park Drive, which separates the hills from the creek. As many as two hundred of the 6-inch-long salamanders have been counted as road kills in a single day along the drive, and the park now closes a 2-mile-long stretch of the roadway during mating season.

January is the peak of the mating season, and while you may not see hundreds of the brown-backed and orange-bellied amphibians on a visit to Tilden Park, you will at least see dozens as they navigate their way between bicyclists and roller-bladers on the asphalt.

Although Tilden Park is the only one that has taken such drastic measures as closing down roads during mating season, many more newts can be seen in another regional park district unit. Briones Regional Park near Lafayette in Contra Costa County has hundreds of breeding pairs of newts that congregate around small ponds in the hills of the park. To see these mating pairs, however, you must take at least a 2-mile hike to their breeding grounds. You reach these from the Briones Road trailhead off Alhambra Valley Road near Martinez on the north side of this large wilderness park. Since the location of the largest congregations of mating newts varies from year to year, call (510) 525-2233 for current information about where to see the largest concentrations of newts, as well as about the naturalist-led hikes to see the newts.

For more information on seeing this natural phenomenon in Tilden Park call (510) 635-0135 or simply take Wildcat Canyon Road to the junction with South Park Drive, park your car and walk along the road or Wildcat Creek. You are more likely to see newts while it is raining, so get out that slicker and find out why the newt crosses the road.

FEBRUARY

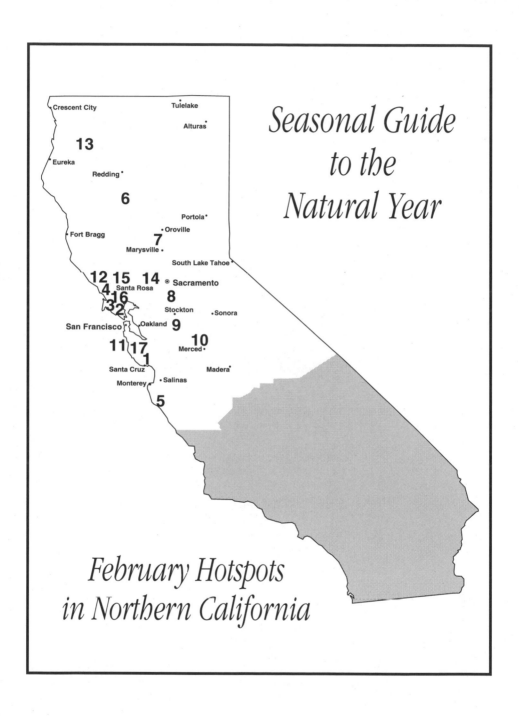

Seasonal Guide to the Natural Year

Crescent City

Tulelake

Alturas

13

Eureka

Redding

6

Portola

Oroville

Fort Bragg

7

Marysville

South Lake Tahoe

12 15 14 Sacramento

Santa Rosa

4

16

8

Stockton

Sonora

3 2

Oakland **9**

San Francisco

11 17

10

Merced

1

Santa Cruz

Madera

Salinas

Monterey

5

*February Hotspots
in Northern California*

MAP SITE KEY

1. Big Basin SP
2. Mount Tamalpais SP
3. Muir Woods National Monument
4. Point Reyes National Seashore
5. Julia Pfeiffer Burn SP
6. Woodson Bridge SRA
7. Colusa SRA
8. Consumnes River Preserve
9. Caswell SP
10. McConnell SRA
11. Butano SP
12. Armstrong Redwoods State Reserve
13. Grizzly Creek Redwoods SP
14. Silverado Trail
15. River Road and Alexander Valley—Sonoma County
16. CA 1 from Stinson Beach north
17. Año Nuevo State Reserve

February Observations

7

Winter Waterfalls of the Coast Range

Each year millions of tourists flock to Yosemite National Park in the Sierra Nevada to watch its waterfalls. These are frozen solid during midwinter, however, and it is still several months before they begin thundering down the granite cliffs. For those who like waterfalls and don't want to wait for the snows to melt to observe them, the hidden canyons of the Coast Range are the answer.

After the heavy winter rains seasonal creeks that are unnoticed during the summer and fall begin to fill. As they do, hundreds of waterfalls begin to tumble over large boulders and steep drops. Most of these are quite small and drop no more than 5 to 10 feet, but there are a number—most of which are far from any roads and hidden to all but the most adventuresome—that any waterfall fancier would appreciate. These drop from 50 to 100 feet and cascade over rocks and cliffs to form pools at the bottom.

These falls are for those who like strenuous hikes and are in good enough condition to take them. These hikes, from 1 to 13 miles one way, are not for the meek, but the waterfalls that are found at the end of them make these winter outings a delightful wilderness experience.

HOTSPOTS

Since most of these falls are located in remote regions of parks it is a good idea to contact park headquarters for maps and current information about the trails before heading out. Be prepared for cold, damp conditions on the hikes, for most are in redwood forests where the tall trees keep all but the barest amount of sunlight from filtering through.

Berry Creek Falls in **Big Basin SP**, a 20,000-acre state park located in Santa Cruz County, is one of the most spectacular falls in the region. It drops 60 feet as it cascades over a series of fern- and moss-covered steps on its way to a large pond at the bottom. You must hike 5.5 miles on the Skyline to the Sea Trail from Waddell Beach on CA 1 to reach this isolated jewel, and if you are up to another mile you come to the smaller, but still impressive, **Cascade Falls**. Call the park headquarters at (408) 338-6132 for a trail map of the park before you take the hike.

Cataract Falls in **Mt. Tamalpais SP** is a series of small falls along Cataract Creek. You can reach the falls by climbing up a steep section of Cataract Trail for about .5 mile from the dam at Alpine Lake on the north slope of Mt. Tamalpais, or you can make a 3.5-mile loop on the **Benstein/ O'Brien/Cataract Trails** from above the falls. The latter route leads through some interesting vegetation types that grow on the serpentine soil of the area. To reach the trailhead take CA 1 off U.S. 101 at the Stinson Beach exit. After 3 miles turn right on the Panoramic Highway and continue to Pantoll Road. Turn right on Pantoll until it dead-ends at Ridgecrest Boulevard. Park at the Rock Springs Picnic Area and take the Benstein Trail downhill from there to the O'Brien Trail, where you turn left. Follow the O'Brien Trail to Cataract Trail along Cataract Creek. Follow the creek back uphill to the picnic area. The falls are along this section of trail.

Alamere Falls in **Point Reyes National Seashore** are unusual falls in that they drop over steep cliffs directly into the Pacific Ocean. The Coastal Trail to the falls (6 miles one-way) leads over marine terraces that have the feel of British moors. By February the hillsides above are covered with a green carpet of grass, and spring wildflowers are beginning to add splotches of color. You reach the trailhead by taking CA 1 off U.S. 101 at the Stinson Beach exit. Follow CA 1 to Stinson Beach and continue north for another 4.5 miles. At the north end of Bolinas Lagoon the Bolinas-Fairfax Road joins with CA 1, and you take a left at the junction. Beware—the residents of Bolinas have an ongoing war with the highway department and remove highway signs to the town as soon as they are put up. Follow Bolinas-Fairfax Road for 1.25 miles along the west side of the lagoon to Mesa Road. Turn right on Mesa and go about 4 miles to Point Reyes National Seashore. Continue past the U.S. Coast Guard Station and the Palomarin Field Station of the Point Reyes Bird Observatory to the end of the paved road. Continue another mile over dirt road to the trailhead.

McWay Falls in **Julia Pfeiffer Burns SP** also fall directly into the Pacific Ocean as they slip over a craggy cliffside in Big Sur. This site is easy to reach, and is located alongside CA 1 about 40 miles south of Monterey.

Hundreds of smaller falls form each year during the rainy season in the Coast Range where seasonal creeks reach their peak in February. You can see these on just about any hike or drive through the region.

8

Walking Among the Willows

At least six types of willows—plus Fremont cottonwood, a close relative—grow along river and creek banks in Northern California and provide us with an unexpected color display in February each year. Don't expect this display to be as brilliant as the later carpets of poppies and lupine that will cover the hillsides of this region, for you will surely be disappointed. If you like your colors more subtle and less splashy, however, you are in for a pleasant surprise.

Riparian forests once covered large areas in Northern California, but the need for lumber to build the burgeoning cities of the nineteenth century and the push for more highly productive farmland as the population increased caused many acres of these forests to be cleared. While the dominant riparian forests in the region were valley oak forests, these always included large numbers of willows in their understories. As the oak were cleared for timber and farmland the willow were also cleared. Unlike the oaks, however, the willows quickly grew back.

Today there are only a small percentage of the original 800,000 acres of valley oak riparian forest standing. The best stand is being jointly protected by the federal government and The Nature Conservancy in the 18,000-acre

Alder catkins add another texture and color to willow thickets in February and March.

Sacramento River NWR near Chico, but public access to the area is limited. The Conservancy's Consumnes River Preserve between Sacramento and Stockton is much smaller, but more accessible for those who want to explore a riparian forest that is much as it was before the Europeans settled California.

You don't have to look far to find a large stand of willow, though, for all you have to do is drive or walk along just about any waterway. Just look at a map, find a creek, river or large marshy area, and you will be surprised as you take a close look during midwinter.

New plant growth starts early in Northern California. When large portions of the nation are still covered with snow and ice the plants in riparian habitats here are beginning to show new growth. For the willow, the first sign that spring is near is the sprouting of new wood on last year's limbs. This new growth adds subtle colors to the darker old growth before new leaves begin to bud out. The new bark is light green on some, dark red on others and bright orange-yellow on still others.

When these are combined they give the willow thickets a slightly fuzzy look from afar, and only as you get closer can you begin to differentiate the colors. With the exception of the bright orange-yellow bark of some willows, none of the colors are brilliant, but together they form a welcome indicator that the blossoms of spring are soon to open.

As the month progresses the thickets take on another, even fuzzier, look. The colors of the new bark slowly become muted, and the buttons, buds and catkins that appear before the new leaves erupt add a cottonlike appearance to the whole tree. This is replaced by the green of new leaves as the month comes to a close.

HOTSPOTS

As I noted earlier, you don't have to search far for this subtle spectacle. Just find a stream or marsh and look closely at the willow that grows alongside the water. If you want an up close look at these, however, there are a number of spots in the region where you can hike among the willow thickets and enjoy the subtle colors.

Woodson Bridge SRA is a small park on the Sacramento River near Corning. Take the Corning exit off I-5 and go 6 miles east on South Avenue to the Sacramento River.

Colusa SRA is located on the banks of the Sacramento River near downtown Colusa. Take CA 20 into Colusa from either the south or west and follow the signs to the state recreation area on the banks of the Sacramento River.

The **Consumnes River Preserve** is operated by The Nature Conservancy and is located south of Sacramento off I-5. Take the Twin Cities Road exit off I-5 22 miles south of Sacramento and follow it east to Franklin Boulevard. Turn south on Franklin Boulevard and go 1.5 miles to the parking area near the trailhead of a self-guided nature trail. The trail is about 5 miles round-trip, but you can hike as little as you want for there is a large stand of willow within the first half mile.

Caswell SP is another area of protected valley oak riparian forest. It is located off CA 99 near the town of Ripon, south of Stockton. Take the Ripon exit off CA 99 and follow Austin Road 6 miles south to the park entrance.

McConnell SRA is located off CA 99 on the Merced River near Ballico. Take Livingston-Cressey Road northeast out of Livingston for 2 miles to the park entrance on the Merced River.

9

Redwood Wildflowers

As the winter rains reach their peak in February the cold Arctic storms lose their hold on the north coast of California. This heralds the beginning of spring in the redwoods. While we generally think of spring as a riot of color as wildflowers begin to cover hillsides, this is far from the case, for the wildflowers like the dark and dank understory of the giant redwoods and Douglas fir that stand high above the canyons and slopes of the Coast Range all the way from Santa Cruz to the Oregon border.

Few people venture into these forests during the winter, preferring to wait until the dampness has passed after the winter rains cease. The few who do venture into them this month, however, are delighted to find plenty of small, muted flowers that add delicate tints to the browns and greens of the forest floor.

Fetid adder's-tongue lily is one of the earliest, and most unusual, of the redwood forest spring flowers. This small lily has a brown flower distinctive for one thing—its fetid odor that draws insects who help it pollinate. Soon after the adder's-tongue come wake robin, giant trillium, redwood sorrel, miner's lettuce and huckleberry. None of these is particularly showy by itself, but together they bestow splotches of color to the dark understory of the redwood forests.

By the end of the month you will see the first blooms of wild ginger, if you get down on your knees and lift up the large, glossy green leaves of the ground-hugging ginger. As you are on your knees you may also want to search for the graceful pink flowers of the calypso orchid that begin to open near the end of February. This member of the orchid family is relatively rare, but worth the search.

The delicate, small, star-shaped blooms of the wild cucumber begin to appear on the vines as they climb up shrub plants near the end of the month, and at about the same time the small yellow and purple blossoms of the redwood violets begin to peek through the debris on the forest floor.

HOTSPOTS

Step into any redwood forest in February and you will be able to spot some, if not all, of the flowers mentioned above. The best spots to look for them, though, are on off-the-track trails in lightly visited redwood state parks. Few people visit the parks during the rainy season and you may have the trails to yourself. Wear warm clothes that will protect you from the damp of the understory, and you may even want to bring a change of clothes for the drive home.

A hand lens helps you enjoy the beauty of the lilliputian blooms of many of the plants.

Butano SP is an off-the-beaten-path park in the Santa Cruz Mountains. You reach it from CA 1 on Pescadero Road. Follow Pescadero Road for 2.5 miles to Cloverdale Road, where you turn south. Continue for another 4.5 miles to the park entrance. Get a park trail map from the rangers and ask where the best wildflowers are.

Armstrong Redwoods State Reserve is reached from U.S. 101 by taking CA 116 at the Cotati exit. Head west through Sebastopol for another 16 miles to Guerneville. At the four-way stop in Guerneville continue straight for another 2.2 miles to the park entrance. Park outside the entrance and walk into the park. You will see wildflowers

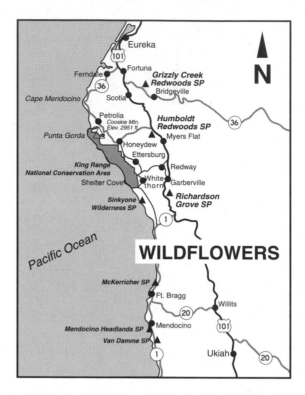

near all the trails that wind through the floor of the park, or you can obtain a park trail map and hike some of the trails that take you to the higher ridges.

Grizzly Creek Redwoods SP is the most inland of all the redwood parks in Northern California and sits along the Van Duzen River near Carlotta. Take CA 36 east from U.S. 101 at Alton south of Fortuna and follow it for about 5 miles to Carlotta and then another 15 miles to the park entrance.

These are just a few of the county, state and national parks that protect the redwoods, and any—even the most heavily visited, such as **Muir Woods National Monument**—offer excellent opportunities to view the small and muted blooms of spring wildflowers found on the floor of redwood forests.

Muir Woods National Monument is reached by CA 1 off U.S. 101. Take the Stinson Beach exit just past Sausalito and follow the signs to Muir Woods.

10

Mustard Galore

The transition from the muted colors of spring wildflowers of the redwood forests to the wild and riotous bright yellow carpets of wild mustard is a shock to the system, but that is just what you can get as you travel inland from redwood country. Mustard—along with two other exotics, Scotch broom and acacia, that thrive in the inland valleys of the coast range—is often an overwhelming visual stimulus when you come upon a carpeted field unexpectedly.

Folklore has it that mustard was first brought to California when one of the mission priests spread mustard seeds along the trail as he walked from mission to mission. But the more prosaic history of the introduction of this European weed to America is that immigrants brought seeds to this country at the end of the nineteenth century as a cover crop for fallow fields, where it was grown and plowed under for its nutrient values. Whichever story is true, there is no doubt that this plant has spread to almost all disturbed fields of the coastal valleys of Northern California, as well as to many other areas. Hay fields, orchards and vineyards all become pallets of yellow blossoms as the 3-foot-tall mustard plants erupt each February.

Among the carpets of yellow are occasional splotches of white. These are patches of wild radish, a close cousin of mustard. Combined, the two make for one of the most visible wildflower displays to be found in Northern California. Nothing else covers such vast areas or is so brilliant in color.

As mustard spreads over large fields, the bright yellow blooms of the acacia begin to break out along roadways. This fast-growing exotic is the first, and most brilliant, blooming tree to erupt each year, and is a perfect complement to the low-lying mustard.

Another exotic, Scotch broom is a shrub plant that grows on open hillsides. Its later blooms match those of mustard and acacias in both color and brilliance.

It is difficult to drive along the roadways of the inland coastal valleys without encountering one or more of these three plants, but there are some especially good drives where you see them all.

HOTSPOTS

The **Silverado Trail** leads up the east side of the **Napa Valley**, where vast vineyards offer prime mustard-growing areas, ranch roads are lined with planted acacia and the wild hillsides are covered with patches of Scotch broom late in the month. From downtown Napa take CA 121 about 1 mile to the junction with the Silverado Trail, and turn north. Follow the trail about 18 miles to Calistoga at its north end. This drive with its great mustard display has become so popular that several organizations in the Napa Valley, with Eastman Kodak as a prime sponsor, have joined together for a two-month-long Napa Valley Mustard Celebration each year in February and March.

Alexander Valley is another grape-growing region where mustard makes a color splash each February. Take Alexander Valley Road off U.S. 101 north of Healdsburg and go about 5 miles to the small crossroads of

Jimtown (you may want to stop in this historic store for a look-see) where you take a left on CA 128. Turn and follow CA 128 north until it returns to U.S. 101 at Geyserville. This is about a 10-mile drive.

CA 1 from Stinson Beach to Bodega Bay is also a good drive in late February and early March for those who want to see an abundance of Scotch broom, along with a number of fields of mustard and an occasional grove of acacia.

11

February
Shorttakes

DRIFTWOOD GATHERING

By February, winter storms have fed the roaring rivers of the North Coast, and piles of driftwood have been sent out into the ocean, only to be deposited along the long beaches. During breaks in the storms, you can walk along beaches from Monterey County to the Oregon border in search of just the right piece of driftwood for your home or garden. The farther north you go, the more driftwood you will find.

RIVER WATCHING ALONG THE NORTH COAST

This is also a good time to watch rivers rushing toward the ocean. California rivers are lackadaisical streams much of the year, but they become wide, roaring rivers after the bulk of the winter rains have fallen. During this period, they often rise above their banks and flood surrounding country.

BLOOMING ORCHARDS
IN THE SACRAMENTO/SAN JOAQUIN VALLEY

By mid-February the peach, almond and other orchards that abound in the Central Valley burst into a riot of pink and white blooms. Several locales have blossom tours where you can see the best displays.

12

Breakout: Elephant Seals

Año Nuevo State Reserve has windswept sand dunes, ridges of mudstone that are turned into wild sculptures by the surf and huge black mounds formed by polychaete worms. In addition, the Christmas Bird Count here ranks among the top twenty in the nation each year.

Most people, however, come to this lonely stretch of CA 1 between Half Moon Bay and Santa Cruz during January and February to see a spectacle found nowhere else in the state. Three-ton male elephant seals begin to arrive at the Año Nuevo beach in December and January each year, with pregnant females following a short time later. By mid-January the females have given birth to young they conceived the previous year. Within a month they are ready to conceive again, and that is the prime time to visit the reserve.

The gigantic males bellow, fight and scuffle as they attempt to gain dominance and the choice of breeding females. This all takes place near the nursing mothers and young that have just been born, and it truly is a primitive spectacle. There is something primeval about the confrontations that tugs at our own hidden, primitive desires, and thousands of people come each year to see this event.

A female elephant seal relaxes on the beach.

So many people visit that you must reserve a ticket to view the scene, which takes place on an isolated section of beach south of Cascade Creek. The guided tour to the beach is about 3 miles round-trip.

You can call the park at (415) 879-0227 for information about the park, but you must call MISTIX at (800) 444-7275 for tour reservations.

MARCH

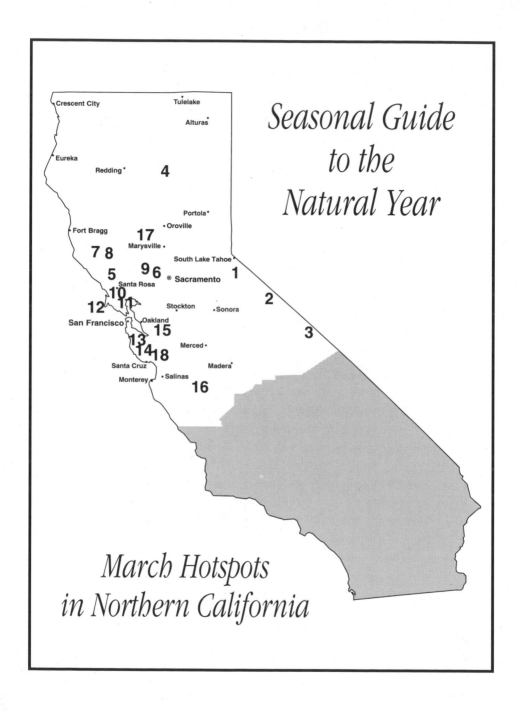

Seasonal Guide
to the
Natural Year

Crescent City
Tulelake
Alturas
Eureka
Redding
4
Portola
Oroville
Fort Bragg
17
Marysville
7 8
South Lake Tahoe
5 **9 6** ◉ Sacramento **1**
Santa Rosa
2
10
Stockton
Sonora
12 **11**
3
San Francisco
Oakland
15
13
Merced
14 18
Santa Cruz
Madera
Monterey
Salinas
16

March Hotspots
in Northern California

MAP SITE KEY

1. Grover Hot Springs SP
2. Travertine Hot Springs
3. Hot Creek
4. Lassen Volcanic NP
5. Lake Sonoma
6. Lake Berryessa
7. Lake Mendocino
8. Clear Lake
9. Annadel SP
10. Coleman Valley Road
11. Burdell Mountain-Olompali State Historic Park
12. Chimney Rock-Point Reyes National Seashore
13. San Bruno Mountain County and State Park
14. Edgewood County Park
15. Black Diamond Mines Regional Park
16. Pinnacles National Monument
17. Gray Lodge Wildlife Area
18. Stevens Creek

March Observations

13

Hot Springs in the Winter

The hot springs that dot the eastern slopes of the Sierra Nevada and southern Cascades are reminders that eastern California is a very geologically active and young region. Mt. Lassen erupted between 1914 and 1917, and a violent earthquake that shook the entire Sierra Nevada range soon after the gold rush lifted some peaks as much as 3 feet. Today earthquakes in the Mammoth Lakes area to the east of Yosemite are frequent and strong—so frequent and strong that the U.S. Geological Survey even issued a volcano alert for the region in the 1980s.

The same geological actions charge the hot springs of the region. These rise from faults and vents where surface water seeps down into fractures. There it comes into contact with super-heated rocks, and the water is pushed back to the surface by the steam formed below. This is the origin of hot springs with temperatures that range from tepid to near boiling.

A near-cult has formed among hot spring users in the West during the past several decades, and there have even been several guidebooks to all the springs where people can take a dip. Over the years some of these springs have become very developed (i.e. Grover Hot Springs SP), while

Bathers enjoy the hot springs on Hot Creek with snow in the background.

others remain little developed, little used funky places where adventurous sorts go to enjoy an unusual natural outing.

The absolute best time of year to enjoy these wonders is toward the end of winter when the snowpack has melted enough so you can reach the springs, but enough snow-banks remain so you can soak in the hot waters and quickly jump into the snowbanks that surround the springs.

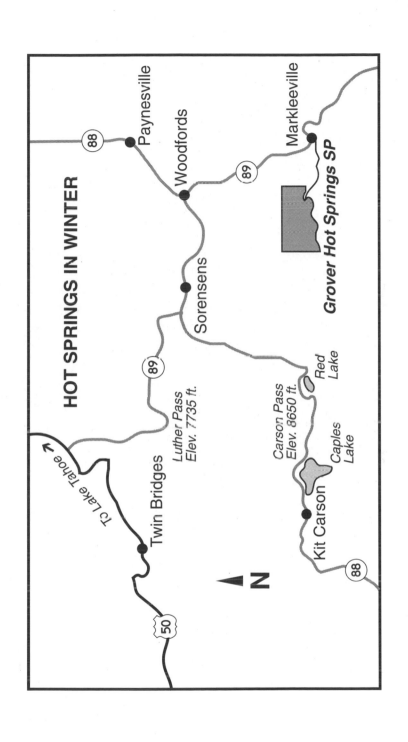

HOTSPOTS

Grover Hot Springs SP outside Markleeville is a developed site where the hot waters are piped into several large swimming pools. The pools are maintained at steady temperatures as water is circulated and replaced regularly. You reach Grover Hot Springs by Taking CA 89 10 miles from U.S 50 near South Lake Tahoe to its junction with CA 88. Take a left on CA 88, go 6 miles to Woodsford, and turn right on CA 4. Continue for 7 miles to Markleeville. From Markleeville take Hot Springs Road west and follow the signs to the park entrance.

Travertine Hot Springs is located off U.S. 395 south of Bridgeport. Over the years volunteers have hand built several pools among the narrow ridges of travertine that rise as much as 8 feet above the surrounding flats. The area is dotted with hot springs, some of which feed the pools. These run quite slowly, and it is easy to regulate the temperature. There is not as much snow in this area as others, but that makes it easier to reach the springs. You get to them by turning east off U.S. 395 onto a dirt road about a half mile south of Bridgeport. If you pass the U.S. Forest Service office you have gone too far. The springs are about a mile off U.S. 395, but you must be careful at several turns. Soon after you turn off the main highway the dirt road makes a 90 degree bend and dead-ends at a maintenance station. Go straight ahead at the bend, and follow a dirt road up a hill past the signs and turnoff to the Bridgeport Borrow Pit (dump). You will see whitish salt deposits on the hills to your right. About a half mile past the Borrow Pit there are parking lots and the first of the pools. Beware—in severe winters you may need a four-wheel-drive vehicle to reach these, and even then you may have some difficulties.

Hot Creek is located just east of Mammoth in the Long Valley Caldera. At the western end of the caldera Hot Creek Gorge contains boiling hot springs and periodic geyser eruptions. The forest service maintains walkways around the hot springs and a dressing room near the parking lot. There are several pools here that vary in temperature. You reach Hot Creek by turning east on Owens River Road from U.S. 395 about 3 miles south of the turnoff to the Mammoth ski resorts. The parking lot is about a mile off U.S. 395.

Although there are no hot springs to soak in at the Sulphur Works in **Lassen Volcanic NP** I have included this hotspot because of the winter snowshoe trips sponsored and led by the park rangers during the winter. This two-hour trek begins at the Lassen Chalet parking lot at an elevation of about 7,000 feet. The trek ends at the thermal pools at the Sulphur Works. These fumaroles form a dramatic scene as the steam rises against the backdrop of snow-covered slopes during the cold of winter. The fumaroles appear more active in the cold air because more clouds are formed as the steam hits the cold air. The chalet is at the south entrance to the park on CA 89 about 52 miles east of Red Bluff. Call the park at (916) 595-4444 for more information about time and dates of these tours.

14

Wild Turkeys in Strut

Wild turkeys are not indigenous to California, but during the 1950s and 1960s the California Department of Fish and Game introduced them into various sections of the state as a game bird. This introduction has been extremely successful, and during March you can see them strut in their courtship display at several locations around northern California.

Wild turkeys have little in common with the domestic turkeys that are grown strictly for their meat. Instead of the domestic animals that have been known to drown in a rainstorm while looking up at the falling rain, wild turkeys are wily, smart birds that are known for their ability to evade hunters—so wily that Ben Franklin urged congress to name them the national bird. Legend has it that he fell only one vote short of succeeding.

Other than during hunting season they are often seen in large flocks, although their muted coloration blends in very well with the grass-covered hillsides and oak forests where they choose to live.

If you are lucky enough to spot the flocks during March you will see a courtship display where the males strut about with their tail feathers spread wide to establish their own territory and attract the females.

HOTSPOTS

Lake Sonoma is a U.S. Army Corps of Engineers project in Sonoma County with several thousand acres of open land between the two arms of the lake. Wild turkeys have flourished in this protected environment and each spring put on marvelous mating displays as they do their mating strut. You reach Lake Sonoma by taking the Dry Creek Road exit off U.S. 101 in Healdsburg and heading west. The visitors' center is located at the base of Warm Springs Dam about 12 miles from Healdsburg. Stop there for directions to the most likely trails where you can see wild turkeys.

Lake Berryessa is another U.S. Army Corps of Engineers project, this one in Napa County. There are fewer developed trails on the slopes that surround the lake, but this means fewer people explore the desolate areas where the wild turkeys thrive. You reach the park headquarters and visitors' center by taking CA 121 north out of Napa for about 15 miles to its junction with CA 128 at Moskawite Corners. Turn left onto CA 128 and continue about 5 miles to Berryessa/Knoxville Road. Turn right and continue about 3 miles to the visitors' center. Find out about the best locations for seeing wild turkeys from the rangers.

Lake Mendocino is yet another U.S. Army Corps of Engineers project with plenty of wild land where the turkeys can roam freely. You reach the visitors' center at the lake by following the signs off U.S. 101 just north of Ukiah. The center is at the base of Coyote Dam on Lake Mendocino Drive. The rangers can give you directions to the most likely spots to see the turkeys in strut.

Wild turkeys are not the only exotic animals found around these lakes. Feral pigs descended from early escapees from both Spanish explorers and early European settlers in the region have flourished in this land of oaks and grass. You will see evidence of these even if you don't see pigs themselves. They often plow up whole hillsides of grass in their search for food, and it is hard to mistake the results for anything else.

15

Coastal Wildflowers

California can be said to have a seven-month spring if spring is the time wildflowers bloom. With six different life zones, the 200 or so miles between the Pacific coast and the ridge of the Sierra Nevada are the equivalent of traveling from Mexico to northern Canada. Toss in the moderating influences of the waters of the Pacific, and you begin to have fantastic wildflower blooms as early as March each year. The succeeding months bring other blooms across the state, as each life zone has its own distinctive flowers. There is even a continuum of blooms from Big Sur in the south to the colder areas in the redwood country near the Oregon border.

The northern coastal regions have the muted wildflowers that grow on the floor of the damp, dark redwood forests in February. By March there are brighter blooms—although not nearly as splashy as those to come in later months—along the open meadows and hillsides along the coast.

Brilliant yellow swatches of Scotch broom cover large areas of open hillsides during early March and are joined by other bright blooms of star lilies, mission bells, brodiaea, red maids and blue larkspur, among others. These combine to cover the slopes near the coast with splotches of color that contrast with the emerald green of the new grass that came with the winter rains. The yellow and blue blossoms of bush lupine add their color later in the month.

These brilliant displays begin earliest near the coast in the regions around Big Sur and slowly move north and inland as the month progresses. By mid-March there are colorful displays in all the inland valleys as far north as Mendocino County and in parts of the Sacramento Valley and the lower foothills of the Sierra Nevada.

HOTSPOTS

A drive around **Clear Lake** in Lake County about an hour north of San Francisco takes you through vast fields of wildflowers. You will also see bright shrubs with dark red blooms along many sections of the route. These are redbud, a local plant that adds plenty of color each spring. The best sections of the route are CA 20 between Nice and Clearlake Oaks on the northeast side of the lake and Lakeview Road and Soda Bay Road on the southwest side.

Annadel SP is on the eastern outskirts of Santa Rosa, and there are several entrances to the park. One is from Spring Creek County Park in Santa Rosa. You get there by taking the CA 12 exit off U.S. 101 in Santa Rosa. Stay on the freeway until it ends at Farmers Lane, and continue straight ahead on Hoen Avenue. Follow Hoen until it ends at Summerfield Road. Across Summerfield, Hoen becomes Newanga. Continue straight on Newanga to the park entrance, go past the dam and park in the parking lot. Spring Creek Trail leads south out of the parking lot and picnic area into Annadel SP.

The next entrance is off Channel Drive in east Santa Rosa. Follow the above directions to Summerfield Road, but turn left on Summerfield instead of going straight. Follow Summerfield until it dead-ends at Montgomery Drive and turn right on Montgomery. Go for about a mile to Channel

Drive and turn right. Continue on Channel for 2 miles to the park entrance. The **W. P. Richardson Trail** leads out of the rear of the parking lot.

The third entrance is off CA 12 about 7 miles east of Santa Rosa. Turn south on Lawndale Road off CA 12 between Oakmont and Kenwood and go just over a mile to the **Lawndale Trailhead**.

All of these trailheads lead into the maze of trails that crisscross Annadel SP, and you can walk as much or as little as you like on any of them. All have excellent flower displays during late March.

You can pick up a trail map to the park at the ranger headquarters that is located on Channel Drive just before the parking lot for the W. P. Richardson Trailhead.

Coleman Valley Road in Sonoma County does not have the extensive fields of blossoms that some of the other hotspots have, but it has one outstanding feature. As you wind through the open pastureland of large sheep ranches you will see small fields of wildflowers, but after you go over the summit where the wide expanse of the Pacific Ocean captures your attention keep an eye out on the uphill side of the road. Large patches of coastal iris can be seen there in full bloom.

There are few other places in the state where you can see such wonderful displays of this lovely flower, but one is nearby. When Coleman Valley Road dead-ends at CA 1 take a left and continue north for just over 4 miles until you come to the entrance to the parking lot at **Shell Beach** on the left. Take the **Kortum Trail** north from the parking lot across the grasslands that cover the marine terrace and you will encounter other large patches of iris.

You get to Coleman Valley Road by taking CA 12 (Bodega Highway) west out of Sebastopol for 5 miles to the village of Freestone. Turn right onto Bohemian Highway and follow its winding route to the community of Occidental. Coleman Valley Road heads west off Bohemian Highway in the middle of town. It is just over 4 miles to CA 1 from Occidental.

Burdell Mountain in **Olompali State Historic Park** is about a mile north of Novato off U.S. 101. You cannot enter the park from U.S. 101 going north, but must make a U-turn at the next turnoff and head back south to the park entrance. Go to the ranger station and visitors' center for a trail map of the park. Head for the trails on the south side of the park for the best displays. This will be about a 3-mile round-trip hike.

The area around **Chimney Rock** in **Point Reyes National Seashore** has a brilliant display of coastal wildflowers, and you reach it by following Sir Francis Drake Boulevard off CA 1 south of Point Reyes Station to its end at the Chimney Rock parking lot. From the parking lot take the trail out to Chimney Rock. Along this .5-mile-long trail the wildflowers are on brilliant display.

San Bruno Mountain County and State Park is home to many rare and endangered plants and animals, offers excellent vistas of the San Francisco Bay region and is seldom crowded. You reach the parking areas of the park by taking the Guadalupe Canyon Parkway west from U.S. 101 south of San Francisco. Follow the signs to the park. The trails to the peak of San Bruno Mountain begin out of the parking lot to the south of the parkway, while the less strenuous trails begin from the north parking lot. Again, you can hike as much or as little as you like to see the wildflowers, but you can see more with less hiking on the north side of the parkway.

Edgewood County Park lies next to I-280 in San Mateo County south of San Francisco. Take the Edgewood Road exit off I-280 and go east for a mile to the park entrance. You can pick up a park map at the parking lot, but any of the trails offer outstanding views of wildflower displays. Many of the wildflowers here are rare and endemic to the serpentine soil that covers the ridge.

The Black Diamond Mines Regional Park outside Antioch has several thousand acres of grass-covered slopes that have brilliant wildflower displays each year. You can enjoy these by simply viewing the displays on the side of Sommersville Road (which exits off CA 4 in Antioch) as you drive into the park, and then by strolling around the level areas near the parking lot, or you can hike along the several miles of trails that climb up some of the slopes. Trail maps are available at the parking area, or you can get one from the East Bay Regional Park District by calling (510) 531-9300.

Pinnacles National Monument is about 35 miles south of Hollister off CA 25. While the monument is more noted for its geologic wonders, it has some of the best wildflower displays found in Northern California. Follow the signs off CA 25 to the park entrance. The hillsides and open grassland on both sides of the road into the park are carpeted with blossoms during late March, and once you are in the park you can ask the rangers where the best wildflower walks are at the time.

These are a few of the outstanding viewing spots in the region, and just about any road that winds through the hills near the coast will take you through regions where wildflowers stand out against the green hillsides during March.

16

Gray Lodge Wildlife Area

Gray Lodge Wildlife Area was mentioned as one of the prime spots to view wintering Canada geese, but there is much more to the area than that. It is also one of the most active wildlife areas in the state during mating season.

Gray Lodge was one of the largest private hunting clubs in California until the state acquired its 2,540 acres in 1931. Since then, the state has acquired more surrounding farm and ranch land to expand the acreage to 8,400. Today over seventy thousand visitors come to the site each year to view the outstanding concentration of waterfowl and other birds from the 80 miles of roads and levees that crisscross the refuge.

While all the flooded ponds at Gray Lodge are active from the beginning of the fall migration, the area becomes even more active as many of the million ducks begin their spring courtship displays. The dazzling plumage of mallards, gadwalls, northern pintails and cinnamon and green-winged teals add to the elaborate courtship displays exhibited by the males as they lay claim to mates.

The tall cottonwoods that rise above the ponds are dotted with layers of nests. The uppermost nests are those of great blue herons, with black-crowned night herons and snowy egrets below. Courtship displays (the nuptial plum-age of the egrets is most elegant) and other iife in the rookery can be observed from a viewing mound located a discreet distance from the trees.

One of the most colorful residents that nest in the refuge is the reclusive wood duck. More than two hundred nesting boxes that are home to a variety of animals the rest of the year are filled with wood ducks and their young during March and April.

As you walk along the levees or drive along the roads, you will see the beginning of the spring wildflower display that follows the nesting season.

Stop at the small lodge where the visitors'center and museum is located to get a road and trail map of the area, as well as information about current activities that can be viewed.

Gray Lodge Wildlife Area is located just north of the Sutter Buttes (often called the smallest mountain range in the world) in the Butte Sink region. In addition to the vast numbers of waterfowl, sandhill cranes winter here in large numbers. To reach Gray Lodge take CA 99 north from Yuba City for 10 miles to Live Oak. Turn west on Pennington Road (also called North Butte) in Live Oak to Almond Orchard Road. Turn north and continue to refuge entrance. The refuge is about 8 miles from Live Oak.

17

March Shorttakes

APPLE BLOSSOMS

Late March is the time to tour the two major apple-producing regions of Northern California. The first is in the Sierra foothills above Placerville along US 50. This region is known as Apple Hill for its extensive orchards. The second is in Sonoma County, where they raise dozens of varieties of apples that bloom over an extended period of time. Both have excellent blossom tours and Apple Blossom Festivals.

BUDDING OAKS

As the many different species of oak trees begin to bud each spring they provide a display of green. Each species has its own color, with some turning red before the green dominates and others budding out in different hues of green. Together they blanket hillsides with a soft, fuzzy-looking cover as the deciduous oaks blend with the evergreen. These displays are best in the hills to the north of San Francisco and in the Sierra foothills through the gold rush country.

LISTENING TO THE TREE FROGS

As the spring rains slack off, and the weather begins to warm, listen for the sounds of the green tree frogs at night.

Many people, when hearing them for the first time, confuse them with crickets, but if you listen closely you can tell the difference. You can sometimes sneak up on the frogs by following their call and surprise them with a sudden shining of light. Children especially love to do this.

RETURNING BIRDS

This is the month when you will see black-headed grosbeak, varied thrush and California towhee at your feeders as they return from their winter homes.

18

Breakout: Ladybugs at Stevens Creek

Did you ever wonder where ladybugs went when they fly away home? Well, one spot is a hillside above Stevens Creek in the Monte Bello Open Space Preserve in Santa Clara County south of San Francisco.

This is only one of many spots that convergent ladybugs (one of over 125 species of ladybugs found in California) congregate in the Coast Range and foothills of the Sierra Nevada each year, but it is the only one I know of that is easy to reach. Ladybugs return to these sites at higher elevations in May and June as their feeding grounds in the low valleys—where they feed on aphids—dry up and before the temperatures rise into the 100s. There they stay until they hibernate in early winter.

Tens of thousands of ladybugs hibernate together until the weather begins to warm up in late February and early March. They then become very active as they mate. The eggs hatch in April and the larvae eat aphids for about three weeks before they pupate.

During hibernation and mating time the ladybugs cluster together on the stems of tall grasses and on tree trunks near the ground. They are easiest to view during the mating period, and the terrace where they cluster in Monte

Bello is high enough above Stevens Creek to be unaffected by any floods during heavy rains.

To reach this site you take the Page Mill Road exit off I-280 in Palo Alto and go west and south for 7 miles to the parking lot at the Monte Bello Open Space Preserve. From the trailhead take the Canyon Trail that heads to the left out of the lot and head downhill for 1.5 miles. You will pass through open grassland on a single track trail before the trail becomes a well-maintained fire road. Stay on the fire road past a sag pond as it heads downhill.

The ladybugs will be visible on the uphill side of the trail about 200 yards above Stevens Creek.

APRIL

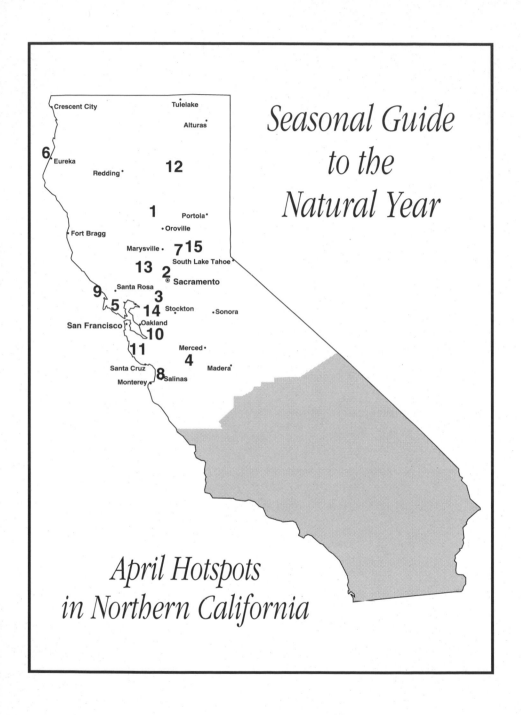

Crescent City

Tulelake

Alturas

6 Eureka

Redding

12

Fort Bragg

1

Portola

Oroville

Marysville

7 15

South Lake Tahoe

13

2

9

Santa Rosa

3

Sacramento

5

14

Stockton

San Francisco

Oakland

Sonora

10

11

Merced

Santa Cruz

4

Madera

Monterey

8 Salinas

*Seasonal Guide
to the
Natural Year*

*April Hotspots
in Northern California*

MAP SITE KEY

1. Vina Plains Preserve
2. Phoenix Park
3. Jepson Prairie
4. Kesterson NWR
5. Audubon Canyon Ranch and Bolinas Lagoon
6. Humboldt Bay NWR
7. Folsom Lake SRA
8. Elkhorn Slough National Estuarine Research
    Reserve
9. Goat Rock
10. San Francisco Bay NWR
11. Bean Hollow State Beach
12. Ash Creek Wildlife Area
13. Sugarloaf Ridge SP
14. Mount Diablo SP
15. Auburn SRA

April Observations

19

Vernal Pools

Great displays of spring wildflowers in Northern California are found around one of the most endangered natural communities in the state. Vernal pools are found in small numbers in other Mediterranean climates around the world, but nowhere are they as diverse as they are in California. Although vernal pools is the name preferred by naturalists, these water-filled shallow depressions have been known as hog wallows, springtime pools, California prairie potholes and holes-in-the-grass-where-wildflowers-grow.

All of these refer to natural communities that can be as small as a few square feet to several acres, are generally found interspersed with grasslands and accumulate water during the rainy season. These pools of standing water form in depressions that lie above an impermeable layer of hardpan. The water, seldom over 2 feet deep, only escapes from the pools by evaporation, which may take from several weeks to several months after the winter rains have ceased.

As the pools slowly shrink, a group of special plants begin to bloom in the newly exposed moist ground. These are visible as rings of white, yellow and blue around the slowly disappearing pools and are composed of some of the rarest and most endangered plants in California. Over two hundred species of plants grow in these unusual communities, many found nowhere else. About half of the plants found around vernal pools do not grow outside California.

These species have adapted to an environment where they must survive extended periods of inundation and desiccation during wet winters and dry summers. Meadowfoam, downingia, crowfoot, mallow, geranium, violet, poppy, primrose and snapdragon are a few of the species that provide the colorful blooms found around the pools. Several species of grasses, including at least nine members of Orcuttieae which are found only in this habitat, provide a backdrop to the profuse blooms of vernal pools.

Vernal pools also provide homes to a diverse fauna. At least five types of fairy shrimp live in them, and the California tiger salamander uses the pools as a breeding ground.

While vernal pools are still found throughout their historic range, only about 5 to 10 percent of their original number survive. This dramatic decrease in numbers has put the plants and animals that depend upon them in jeopardy. Over two dozen plants on California's endangered species list are found only around vernal pools.

Most vernal pools have been destroyed by land being converted to agricultural use. Drainage patterns are altered, and land is then plowed or leveled for farming and ranching. Urban expansion is another major contributor to the loss of the wetlands. In fact, much of the best development land in the Central Valley is in prime vernal pool habitat.

The California Department of Fish and Game and The Nature Conservancy are two major organizations that have protected the best examples of vernal pools left—although others are found in a national wildlife refuge in the lower valley—and you can see why they have made the effort to save these natural phenomena that occur during April each year.

HOTSPOTS

Vina Plains is a Nature Conservancy preserve in Tehama County in the upper Sacramento Valley. The preserve is a rarity in the valley because it has never been plowed, and its 1,950 acres are one of the few patches of virgin grassland left in the state.

April is the prime time to visit the preserve most years, although docent-guided tours are conducted each Saturday and Sunday from the first of March until the middle of May, or until the ponds have dried up. You may be able to arrange to visit the preserve at other times, but you should always check with The Nature Conservancy before visiting any of their preserves. Call the Docent Chair/Tour Coordinator at (916) 891-8462 for information about the tours and about entry to the preserve at other times.

The preserve is located on CA 99 13 miles north of Chico. The entry gate is on the east side of the highway about

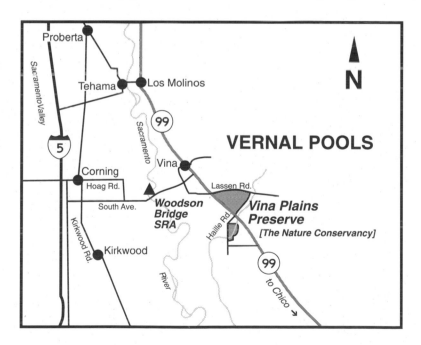

one-third mile north of Singer Creek, which crosses under the highway, and directly opposite Haille Road.

Phoenix Park is a small city park in Orangevale on the outskirts of Sacramento where the Department of Fish and Game has helped protect a small patch of vernal pools that was threatened by housing developments. Developed trails, with foot bridges, lead visitors through the midst of the pools where you can get close-up views of the rings without harming the plants. The park is located on Sunset Avenue about a half mile past Hazel Avenue in Orangevale, and is on the site of an old airport.

Jepson Prairie is another Nature Conservancy preserve and another unplowed grassland. This 1,566-acre preserve is jointly administered by The Conservancy and the Institute of Ecology at the University of California at Davis, and its **Olcott Pond** is one of the largest vernal pools in the world. The Southern Patwin Indians once foraged for food around Olcott. This was in a time when tule elk, pronghorn and grizzly bear roamed in the waving fields of purple needlegrass that grow around the pond. These large animals no longer inhabit the Sacramento Valley, but the spring wildflowers still encircle the pond as it slowly shrinks as warm weather comes to the valley. Docents lead tours to Olcott Pond during the spring, and you can get information on times and dates by calling the Institute of Ecology at (916) 752-6580.

Again, never visit a Nature Conservancy preserve without first contacting the preserve administrator in case access is limited. A drive by the broad fields on CA 113 near Jepson Prairie does give you a good view of vernal pools from the road, however. You reach the preserve from I-80 about halfway between San Francisco and Sacramento. Take CA 113 south off I-80 through Dixon. Continue for 13 miles past the small farming community. At a dogleg with a yellow flashing light where CA 113 goes left, stay to the right. This dirt road is Cook Lane. Stay on the road for three-quarters of a mile and park on the shoulder. The entrance to the preserve is marked with a sign.

Kesterson NWR is more noted for the stir caused when wildlife biologists discovered deformed young waterfowl in the refuge several years ago. The problem was selenium concentrations caused by agricultural runoff. Although this problem has not been completely eliminated, there is still plenty to see at this unit of the **San Joaquin Valley NWR Complex**, including some of the most colorful vernal pools in the state. Visitors to the preserve are limited to drives and hikes along Gun Club Road, which crosses the preserve, and CA 140, which borders it. These give good views of the pools, however. You get to the refuge by taking CA 140 west from CA 99 in Merced for 40 miles, or east from CA 33 from Gustine for just over 5 miles.

20

Heron and Egret Rookeries

Great blue herons are majestic wading birds that stand 4 feet high and have a wing span of 6 feet. Common egrets are only slightly smaller, and together these two species form a remarkable sight as they court, mate and raise their young in rookeries high above the surrounding countryside. These can be in cottonwood trees, as are the rookeries found in the Central Valley, or in tall redwoods as at Audubon Canyon Ranch in Marin County.

The great blue herons begin their courtships sometime in February, and the egrets join with their white courtship plumage about a month later. By April both have built their nests and laid their clutch of eggs. This is a prime time to view these magnificent wading birds. The herons' nests are located in the top of the trees, and the egrets just a bit lower. Both are clearly visible at rookeries where you can view the trees from above, such as Audubon Canyon Ranch, where a trail leads to a ridge that rises above the redwood grove where the herons and egrets return each year to nest.

The large birds frequently fly away from the nests to feed in nearby Bolinas Lagoon, and as they return others rise slowly and circle around the nests on their way to the feeding grounds. This continuous action is accompanied by

Frogs are considered a delicacy by wading birds such as egrets, herons and sandhill cranes

chatter as the birds make room for one another on the nest, and as birds occasionally fight over territory.

By the end of April the first eggs have hatched, and the flights to the feeding grounds become even more frequent as the young birds squawk loudly for food. The rookeries are very busy places full of noise and movement from the time the first hatchlings arrive until the end of summer when the young birds fledge. But the most exciting time to visit is during April when an occasional laggardly couple are still courting, nests are being built, eggs laid and the first babies hatched.

Although the number of rookery sites has decreased in Northern California during the past fifty years, there are still several excellent spots where you can view the frantic activity of herons and egrets during nesting time.

HOTSPOTS

The absolute best spot to view nesting activities of great blue herons and common egrets in Northern California is at **Audubon Canyon Ranch** along the shores of **Bolinas Lagoon**. This preserve is jointly owned and operated by several Audubon Society chapters in the San Francisco area, and its primary purpose is to protect the heron and egret rookery. There are over 175 nests atop 250-foot-tall redwood and fir trees, and visitors can view these from above after a mile hike up a trail that leads through an oak/bay forest. The ranch also operates a nature education center for local schools.

The ranch opens to the public for weekends in early March and stays open until the end of May. It is located on Shoreline Highway (CA 1) three miles north of Stinson Beach. For more information call (415) 868-9244.

You can view herons and egrets from the rookery feeding in the marshes of Bolinas Lagoon as you drive along Shoreline Highway.

California's northernmost heron rookery is located on **Indian Island** in the **Humboldt Bay NWR**. This 2,200-acre refuge is located at the southern end of the state's second largest bay and is one of the prime birding sites in the state. Bring binoculars and spotting scopes for the best views of the rookery. From Eureka you reach the refuge by heading south on U.S. 101 for 11 miles. Take the Hookton exit, then turn right on Eel River Drive. Take a left almost immediately onto Ranch Road Drive and go .5 mile to the refuge gate.

Another island rookery is located at the **Folsom Lake SRA** near Sacramento on Anderson Island in Folsom Lake. This rookery is best viewed from a boat, although you can see activity from shore with binoculars or spotting scopes.

From U.S. 50 east of Sacramento take the Folsom exit, and continue past the town of Folsom to Dam Road. Take a left on Dam Road, pass over the dam and continue to the park headquarters. You can get more information about Anderson Island there.

Farther south there is a rookery at the **Elkhorn Slough National Estuarine Research Reserve**. This reserve is a wetlands along Monterey Bay and is one of nineteen national estuarine research reserves in the nation. Along the South Marsh Loop herons and egrets nest in the top of a grove of Monterey pine. You reach the reserve by heading north on CA 1 from Moss Landing. Take Dolan Road east off CA 1 for 3.5 miles to Elkhorn Road. Turn left on Elkhorn and go 2.5 miles to the reserve entrance. Call (408) 728-2822 for information.

21

Pupping Harbor Seals

Each winter harbor seals haul out of the Pacific at favorite sites and congregate in preparation for pupping. These spotted seals are very common along the Pacific coast, where they forage on medium-sized fish as well as crabs and bivalves. Although salmon fishermen often complain about harbor seals poaching on their catch, research has shown that salmon actually compose a very small percentage of the seals' natural diet.

These seals are most commonly noted for their spotted coat, but the spots disappear when the seals' coats dry as they rest out of the water. You can see small groups of seals sunning themselves at haul-out sites on rocky islets just offshore or on beaches near the mouth of rivers anytime of the year, but there is much more activity during pupping and mating periods.

As the females near pupping both they and males congregate in larger numbers than usual at haul-out sites where food is most abundant. The females were impregnated the previous year and give birth to a single pup soon after they haul out. The pups have a short nursing period, as with most seals, and mating does not occur until the pups have been weaned.

Mating takes place in the water, so you cannot see much of the courtship and mating behavior. Rather, you see a general increase in activity at the haul out sites as the weaned pups begin exploration of their environment, and the courting males and females move in and out of the water much more frequently.

Most of the year harbor seals are timid and enter the water when approached by humans. During pupping and mating time they are not as leery of human intruders, however, and are vulnerable when people come too close to their colonies. The most accessible colonies are in state parks, most of which have volunteers who insure the safety of the young seals by monitoring visitors. Dogs are a particular concern, for they can ravage a colony in a short period of time.

HOTSPOTS

Goat Rock Beach in the **Sonoma Coast State Beaches Complex** is the site of one of the most accessible harbor seal haul-outs along the entire northern California coast. This beach is at the mouth of the Russian River, where food is plentiful for the seals and the inland side of the beach is protected from pounding waves. This perfect pupping ground is also an ideal outing for those who wish to watch the young pups as they nurse and explore their environment. Goat Rock Beach is off California 1 about 10 miles north of the coastal village of Bodega Bay and 1 mile south of the small community of Jenner. Park in the north parking lot and hike across the sandy beach to the haul-out area.

Far to the north there is a haul-out and pupping area in **Humboldt Bay**. The exact location of the haul-out varies from year to year, but a drive west on Hookton Road from U.S. 101 south of Eureka to Table Bluff Road at the south end of the bay should take you past the pupping grounds.

Another good site for viewing mother harbor seals with their pups is **Bolinas Lagoon**. Take the Stinson Beach exit off U.S. 101 in Mill Valley just north of the Golden Gate Bridge and follow CA 1 over Mt. Tamalpais, through Stinson Beach, and north along the east side of the lagoon. About halfway between Stinson Beach and the Bolinas turnoff you will see the harbor seal haul-out.

The **San Francisco Bay NWR** on the east side of San Francisco Bay is another good spot to see harbor seal pups. Take the Thornton Avenue exit at the east end of the Dumbarton Bridge (just before the toll plaza when approaching from the east) and drive 1.5 miles to the refuge entrance. Ask at the interpretive center about the location of the haul-out.

A small population of harbor seals can be seen on rocks just offshore from **Bean Hollow State Beach**. This beach is located along CA 1 about 41 miles north of Santa Cruz and 15 miles south of Half Moon Bay. The seals haul out on different rocks about 100 yards offshore, and can be viewed either with or without binoculars as you hike along a marine terrace above the shoreline.

22

Ash Creek Wildlife Area

Ash Creek is wild, isolated and a place of extremes. Mt. Shasta rises to the north above Big Valley, where Ash Creek Wildlife Area is located, and Mt. Lassen is visible against the southern skyline. Alkali marshes merge with lava flows, and hardy junipers rise above rugged grassland where wildlife abounds. Birders, wildflower enthusiasts and hikers enjoy the serenity offered by this 14,100-acre wildlife area.

Native Americans called the broad valley "God's Smile" and early European settlers named it more simply as Big Valley. In the heart of this broad, flat region sits a 3,000-acre natural wetland known just as simply as Big Swamp. At least six seasonal streams feed this wetland, and wildlife of all sorts comes to feed and drink around its edges. While most of the other natural wetlands in Big Valley were drained with canals and ditches that altered their natural features, Big Swamp was saved by the quick action of a Department of Fish and Game warden who joined with concerned citizens and, unlikely as it may seem, the U.S. Army Corps of Engineers to stop the owners of the property from draining the swamp. In 1986 the Department of Fish and Game purchased the first piece of what is now the Ash Creek Wildlife Area.

Today Ash Creek is one of nine areas that form the California Wildlands Program. A naturalist is assigned to each of these areas to develop programs that will draw people to see the bountiful wildlife in the regions and to learn about the importance of protecting whole habitats.

Sandhill cranes, cackling geese (the smallest subspecies of Canada geese), bald eagles and sage grouse are just a few of the impressive birds seen in the valley. Pronghorn, elk and deer forage in open grassland.

Spring, which begins in April at the 4,000-foot elevation of the valley floor, brings vibrant sounds as nature begins its rejuvenation process. Birds begin their ritual courtship displays, and the air fills with the distinctive drumming sounds of male sage grouse as they raise the feathers on their necks, lift their tails into spiky fans and strut for the females.

Male greater sandhill cranes bow, hop, skip and jump with outspread wings. Their long legs are left dangling on these jumps that are intended to impress unattached females, but the male cranes seem more like gangly adolescent boys trying to impress teenage girls on a school playground.

The common snipe announce their intentions during a courtship flight where their produce eerie, tremulous calls called winnowing.

And these are only the most elaborate displays. White-faced ibises, white pelicans and Great Basin Canada geese are a few more of the numerous waterfowl and wading birds that nest in the wetlands. All of these nesting birds and waterfowl are a powerful attraction to the acrobat of the skies, the peregrine falcon. This rare raptor is also known as the duck falcon from its preference for ducks and other small water birds as food.

All of these commingle at Ash Creek in April as the mating season gets in full swing, and together they provide visitors with a cacophony of sound that accompanies the

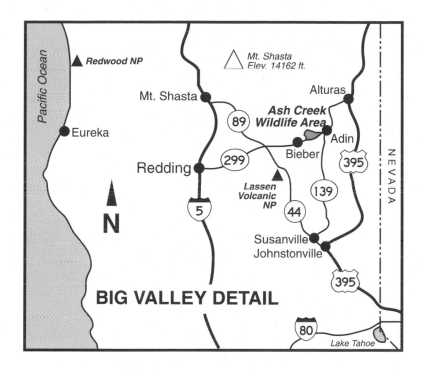

BIG VALLEY DETAIL

visual delights of aerobatic falcons, stately cranes and formations of ducks and geese as they feed in and around the swamp.

And if this isn't enough, if you visit the area in late April after a warm spring you can find other visual treasures. The dull gray of sagebrush hides clusters of larkspur, lupine, camas lilies, scarlet gilia and Indian paintbrush. There are even some small vernal pools in the valley where the bright rings of flowers stand out against the background of sage.

By late April you may also see the first of the rare and beautiful Swainson's hawk as they come to Pilot Butte to nest. This is one of the best places in Northern California to see these strikingly marked raptors nest, for they need plenty of open country to forage. A female has a territory of at least 2,000 acres, and males as much as five times that.

To reach this pristine natural paradise take CA 299 from Redding for about 100 miles to Bieber. Continue on CA

299 east of Bieber for 2.5 miles to the Ash Creek Wildlife Area headquarters. Two roads (County Roads 419 and 429) and five well-spaced parking lots provide excellent roadside viewing of much of the wildlife area, but you can also hike into the area for closer views of the wildlife. There are no marked hiking trails, but it is relatively easy to hike anywhere in the area.

23

April
Shorttakes

GREEN HILLS

The hills of Northern California reach their richest green as the winter rains decrease and the weather warms considerably. This is a good time to explore some of the open grasslands of our parks. That is, if you aren't allergic to the pollens that are carried on the spring winds. Just about anywhere you go you will see the tall grasses swaying in the wind, but you don't realize the diversity of the grasses unless you walk among them.

WATERFOWL HATCHLINGS

If you head for national wildlife refuges in the far northeast corner of the state you will see plenty of waterfowl hatchlings this month. Canada geese are among the first to hatch, and you can see the fuzzy goslings as they swim behind their parents in the wetlands of the refuges.

LAST OF THE RAINS

Enjoy the last of the rains this month, for you aren't likely to see any again until November. By that time you will be looking forward to the wet weather after a summer of heat and dry. Walk in the rain and maybe do a little dancing. Not too many people will think you are crazy.

RISING MOUNTAIN RIVERS

Mountain rivers that were frozen solid only a month or so before are beginning to rise as the snow at higher elevations begins to melt rapidly. This melt quickly reaches the major river systems of the western Sierra, where the torrents rise in the narrow river canyons. This is a good time to watch, but don't get too near. The flows are powerful and frigid.

24

Breakout:
Spring Snakes

People aren't the only animals that head outdoors as the warm weather of spring approaches. Snakes, most of which hibernate during the wet and cold of winter, become active and leave their nests for the warmth of the sunshine. This causes unavoidable confrontations between the two species, confrontations that most people dread, but unnecessarily so.

The rattlesnake is the only poisonous snake found in Northern California, although several subspecies live in the region. Rattlesnake bites can cause serious harm to humans, but few people die from them. Rattlesnakes are seldom aggressive toward humans and generally strike only when cornered or provoked.

Fears and myths about rattlesnakes, and snakes in general, are usually far from the truth. Many people—strange as it may seem to those who are phobic about the creatures—actually look forward to the early warmth of spring so they can hunt for rattlesnakes, as well as other more populous species of snakes that live in Northern California.

And once the warmth of spring has arrived it isn't difficult to find snakes. A walk in any park with plenty of boulders where snakes can lie in the welcome rays of the sun is all you need to find an abundance of garter, gopher, king, ring neck and rubber boa snakes.

The largest of these is the gopher snake, but the most widely seen are the five species of garter snakes found in California. One of the most adaptable of American snakes, garters are found in almost every environment, from abandoned city lots to open fields. They prefer to be near water, though, and are seen throughout the year in many parts of Northern California since they appear to be more cold-tolerant than other snakes.

Garter snakes vary in color, intensity and pattern from region to region, but almost all have bright stripes that run the length of their body. Generally these red to orange stripes are set off by a background of dark gray. Garter snakes bear their young live, but don't expect to see young during the spring—that is when mating occurs. The young are born in late summer.

Garter snakes seldom exceed 36 inches in length, although the rare giant garter snake of the Central Valley may reach as much as 50 inches. If garter snakes were as poisonous as rattlesnakes there would be many more deaths from snakebite. They are aggressive, attack when handled and will bite. These bites seldom break the skin, but do occasionally.

Also frequently seen are the larger gopher snakes that hikers often confuse with rattlesnakes. Longer than most rattlesnakes, gopher snakes have slender bodies that gradually slim down to a pointed tail. Rattlesnakes have much bulkier bodies that abruptly narrow down to the tail. The gopher snake often mimics a rattle if startled. It moves its tail rapidly, as does the rattlesnake, but the sound is only produced when it hits dry leaves or brush. This is enough, however, to convince many people they have encountered a rattler.

Gopher snakes are more active in daytime than many other snakes, except during the high daytime temperatures of summer. Then they become most active at dusk and night.

HOTSPOTS

Whether you are interested in rattlesnakes or the less threatening nonpoisonous snakes found in California, there are several areas in northern California where you are almost guaranteed to find them during the first warm days of spring.

To the north of San Francisco in Sonoma County one of the best places to see snakes is **Sugarloaf Ridge SP**. This park has boulder fields, sunny slopes, creeks, ponds and grasslands where many species of snakes can feed and rest. Sugarloaf is off CA 12 about 10 miles east of Santa Rosa. Turn north on Adobe Canyon Road and continue 2.5 miles up a steep, curvy road to the park entrance. You are likely to see snakes on any of the park trails, but you may want to ask rangers where you are most likely to spot rattlers.

East of San Francisco in Contra Costa County is **Mt. Diablo SP**. This is one of the best snake-hunting areas in all of northern California. This large park features the highest peak in the east bay. Mt. Diablo rises high above the flat Central Valley and Sacramento/San Joaquin Delta to the east and north, and draws thousands of visitors in early spring as the wildflowers bloom on the open hillsides. This is also the best time to see snakes. Take I-680 south from I-80 to Walnut Creek. To reach the north gate of the park take Ygnacio Valley Road east to North Gate Road. continue on North Gate Road to the park entrance. Again all trails are prime snake hunting areas, but you may wish to check with rangers about where to find rattlesnakes.

Snakes, particularly rattlers, are abundant throughout the Sierra Nevada foothills, with their thick cover of chaparral and outcroppings of granite. Two places stand out, however. One is **Folsom Lake SRA**. Trails meander along the shoreline of Folsom Lake and take you through oak grasslands where snakes can enjoy especially fruitful hunting of gophers, mice and voles, yet still be near the water. Trail guides are available at the park headquarters on Dam Road in Folsom. Take Folsom Boulevard north off U.S. 50 to the east of Sacramento. In Folsom continue north on East Natoma Street to Dam Road. Turn west on Dam Road and continue over the dam to the park headquarters.

The other is **Auburn SRA**, which runs along both sides of the American River just to the south of Auburn. Take CA 49 south out of Auburn as it heads down toward the river about 1 mile to the park headquarters. As you pick up a trail guide, you can ask about where you are most likely to spot rattlers.

MAY

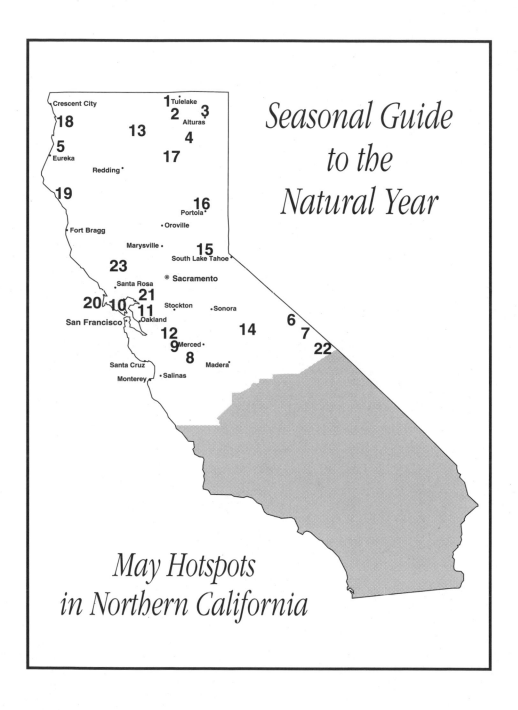

Crescent City

18

5
Eureka

Redding •

19

• Fort Bragg

Marysville •

23

Santa Rosa •

20 **10**
11
San Francisco

Santa Cruz

Monterey

1 Tulelake
2 **3**
Alturas

13

4

17

16
Portola •

• Oroville

15
South Lake Tahoe •

◉ Sacramento

21
Stockton •

Oakland

12
9 • Merced •
8 Madera •

• Salinas

• Sonora

14

6
7
22

*Seasonal Guide
to the
Natural Year*

*May Hotspots
in Northern California*

MAP SITE KEY

1. Klamath Basin NWR Complex
2. Lava Beds National Monument
3. Modoc NWR
4. Ash Creek Wildlife Area
5. Lake Earl Wildlife Area
6. Bodie SP
7. Benton Crossing Road
8. San Luis NWR
9. San Joaquin Valley NWR Complex
10. Ring Mountain Preserve
11. Mount Diablo SP
12. Mount Hamilton
13. McCloud River Preserve
14. Yosemite NP
15. Horsetail Falls
16. Feather Falls
17. McArthur/Burney Falls SP
18. Prairie Creek Redwoods SP
19. Sinkyone Wilderness SP
20. Point Reyes National Seashore
21. Grizzly Island Wildlife Area
22. Owens Valley
23. Boggs Lake

May Observations

25

Western Grebe and Sage Grouse Courtship Dances

Animals are like humans. Each seems to have its own distinct courtship behaviors. Some are sedate and go almost unnoticed, while others are loud, boisterous and can't be missed. Two of the latter are the western grebe and the sage grouse.

Male grebe carry on their courtship dance on the water, where they combine swimming, flying and running along the surface of the water with elaborate feather displays. These are all a prelude to nesting and raising young grebe. The grebe even offer an unusual spectacle after the young hatch.

By early summer grebe hatchlings are found in waterways and wetlands across the state, and the downy hatchlings seldom leave their parents' backs until they are ready to dive on their own. They cling tightly to their parents' backs even during dives for food.

The sage grouse are even more colorful during mating time than the grebe. Males fill air sacks in their chests, fan their tail feathers and strut around in an attempt to attract a mate. As the grouse begin their courting in late spring you will hear loud booming during early morning hours at large clearings in sagebrush country. After the male grouse fill the air sacks in their chests they let loose with booms that can be heard across wide areas of sagebrush country. If you are lucky enough to spot the booming males you will see them fan their tails and stomp their feet before doing a special little extra shuffle to further display their fans.

As the morning passes males begin small fights to gain preferred strutting territory. Two males square off, with each attempting to outdo the other with booms and struts. When neither backs down they move toward each other until their chests touch. At that moment they explode. They go straight up, chest to chest, come back down and chase each other around in a tight circle.

To onlookers it isn't clear how they decide who the winner is, but soon the loser leaves the clearing and the females.

Grouse or grebe. Sage country or marshland. Take your choice, for the courtship displays of both are must-see natural events.

HOTSPOTS

From the wildlife refuges along the Oregon border down the east side of Northern California both sage grouse and western grebe are found in abundance.

In the far northeast corner of the state grebe are found in the **Klamath Basin NWR Complex** that includes **Clear Lake, Tule Lake** and **Lower Klamath NWRs**. These three are located within miles of the Oregon border in marshland of the high desert country of Modoc County. Lower Klamath and Tule Lake have auto tours that take you along the top of levees that reach into the depths of the refuges. There you can get excellent views of courting grebe.

An auto tour of the Lower Klamath NWR takes you through some prime viewing areas. Both a CALTRANS vista point and the beginning of an auto tour are located 9 miles east of U.S. 97 on CA 161. CA 161 is about 25 miles south of Klamath Falls, Oregon. The information plaques at the vista point give you information about the auto tour.

MAY

If you want information about other viewing opportunities in the refuge you can visit the refuge headquarters and visitors' center by continuing east on CA 161 8 miles toward the town of Tulelake to Hill Road. Turn south and go 4 miles to the visitor center. You can call or write the headquarters beforehand for information at Klamath Basin National Wildlife Refuge Complex, Route 1, Box 74, Tulelake, CA 96134; (916) 667-2231.

Just south of the above complex is **Lava Beds National Monument**. Water dominates the refuges, but dry sage that struggles to survive in the rugged lava fields dominates the monument, and it is here that the sage grouse thunders and dances during courtship time.

To reach the monument head south from Tulelake on CA 139 to the crossing of Stonghold. Take CR 111 south for about 1.5 miles to the northeast entrance of the monument. The northern boundary of the monument borders the wildlife refuge and there are several wildlife overlooks near the entrance.

Check at the entrance for the most likely places to spot courting sage grouse or simply head for the monument early in the morning and follow the sounds. You can contact the monument beforehand at P.O. Box 867, Tulelake, CA 96134; (916) 667-2283.

Modoc NWR is courting ground for both sage grouse and western grebe and combines the habitats of Tule Lake and Lava Beds. The Warner Mountains rise in the distance, and ponds are set in the midst of gently rolling sagebrush country.

From Alturas head east on CR 56 to CR 115. Turn south and continue on CR 115 to the refuge headquarters. For more information contact the refuge at P.O. Box 1610, Alturas, CA 96101; (916) 233-3572.

A little farther south is **Ash Creek Wildlife Area** (featured in Chapter 19) where sage grouse are only one of many species of courting birds that are in full display.

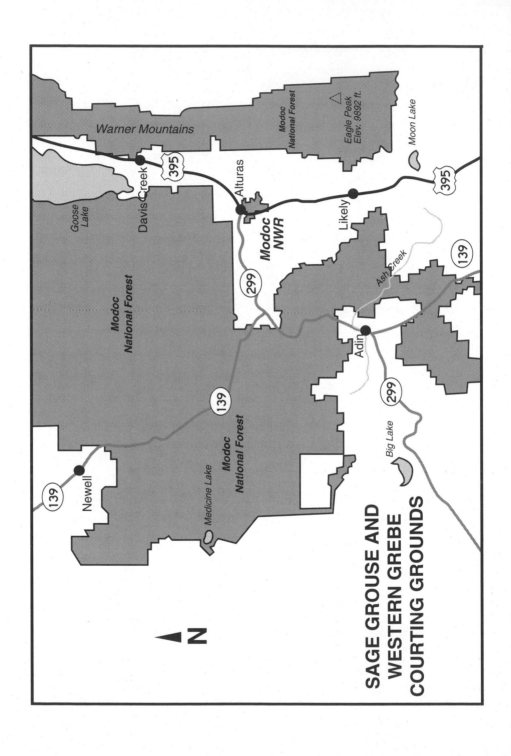

N

SAGE GROUSE AND
WESTERN GREBE
COURTING GROUNDS

Warner Mountains

Modoc National Forest

Eagle Peak Elev. 9892 ft.

Moon Lake

Goose Lake

Davis Creek

Alturas

Modoc NWR

Likely

Ash Creek

Adin

Modoc National Forest

Medicine Lake

Modoc National Forest

Big Lake

Newell

395

299

139

Take CA 299 from Redding for about 100 miles to Bieber and continue east for 2.5 miles to the Ash Creek Wildlife Area headquarters where you can get information on courting grouse. Two roads (County Roads 419 and 429) and five well-spaced parking lots provide excellent roadside viewing of much of the wildlife area, but you can also hike into the area for closer views of the wildlife. There are no marked hiking trails, but it is relatively easy to hike anywhere in the area.

In the far northwestern part of the state grebe conduct their courtship dance at the **Lake Earl Wildlife Area** just outside Crescent City. This large area includes lakes, dunes, upland forests and fields and plenty of seasonal wetlands. Western grebe frequently nest in the northeast corner of the lake, and that is where you will most likely see the courtship dance.

You reach the wildlife area by taking Lake Earl Road north from Crescent City to Old Mill Road. Take a left on Old Mill and continue 1.5 miles to the wildlife area headquarters.

Along the remote eastern slope of the Sierra sits the ghost town of **Bodie**. While most visitors to this isolated park go to view the deserted buildings, others go to hear the drumming sounds of courting sage grouse. The grouse strut down streets where gunfighters once ruled, and the pre-served buildings from gold rush days offer a backdrop to the courtship displays.

Head south on U.S. 395 from Bridgeport for 7 miles. Turn east on Bodie Road and continue for 13 miles on the paved road to the park.

Farther south you can see and hear the courtship display of sage grouse near the junction of **Benton Crossing Road and U.S. 395**. This is 30 miles north of Bishop in open sagebrush country.

The California Department of Fish and Game in Bishop often conducts early morning public tours of the strutting grounds. You can contact them at (619) 871-1171.

Courting grebe can also be seen at the **San Luis NWR**, one of three refuges in the **San Joaquin Valley NWR Complex**. The flat grasslands here are surrounded by tree-lined sloughs and the rambling San Joaquin River. Grebe can be seen in most water-filled areas.

The refuge is 10 miles north of Los Banos in the Central Valley. Take North Mercy Springs Road (CR J14) 8 miles to Wolfsen Road. Turn northeast and continue 2 miles to the refuge. You can drive along the top of the levees in search of the courting grebe.

26

Spring Wildflowers

By May it seems that Northern California has been in bloom forever. In previous months there have been the muted blooms of the redwood forests, the brilliant yellow of mustard and acacia and the magic circles of vernal pools. All were just a prelude to the magnificent displays of blossoms that adorn the hillsides of most of the region this month. The gold of California poppies forms a colorful backdrop for blue lupine, while pink and red blossoms appear as splatters of paint against the green hillsides. Mariposa lily, Indian paintbrush, buttercup, shooting star and spring vetch are other flowers seen this month.

The earlier blooms were just the beginning of California's seven-month spring, leading up to the peak of the season. This month you cannot avoid viewing a display of reds, pinks, blues and yellows as you drive around the region. There are some areas that are even more colorful than others, though, and these are a must-see. From the eastern slopes of the Coast Range across the wide Central Valley to the lower reaches of the foothills that run along the eastern side of the valley there are sites where the number, variety and color of wildflowers astound even the most jaded observers.

Spring wildflowers add color to the green of new grass.

Most of the best wildflower viewing sites are to the west of the Sierra Nevada, but there is one area on the east side that is worth mentioning. Along U.S. 395 for about 4 or 5 miles both to the north and south of Lee Vining and Mono Lake the sagebrush desert is sprinkled with bushes that turn light pink during May. These are the wild desert peach, and it is easy to miss their subtle display. As you drive along the highway, however, you will see an isolated bush that looks different from the others. Then you will begin to notice more and more as you look more closely. If you park alongside the highway and walk into the sagebrush you will then spot more small flowers in bloom along the desert floor.

HOTSPOTS

Several excellent wildflower viewing areas are within easy driving of San Francisco. The closest is **Ring Mountain Preserve** on the Tiburon Peninsula off U.S. 101. Take the

Paradise Drive exit in Corte Madera and follow the drive east for 1.75 miles. As you pass Westward Drive there is a gate and sign on the right. Park off the pavement and walk to the trailhead.

Many of the wildflowers in the preserve grow only on the serpentine soil that lies atop the peninsula and are found in only a few other locations near San Francisco. The views from the top of the trail are stupendous year-round. It is a 2-mile round-trip to the top and back.

Only a little farther away is **Mt. Diablo SP**, where several trails lead through bright splotches of wildflowers during the spring. Mt. Diablo, at 3,849 feet, is the centerpiece of the park, which is located about 20 miles east of Oakland in Contra Costa County. You get to the summit by taking Ygnacio Valley Road east off I-680 in Walnut Creek. At North Gate Road turn south and continue until you reach the parking lot at the top. There is a level, .5-mile trail that circles the peak and an observation deck on top. You will see wildflowers down the slopes of the peak, or you can visit several other trails in the park where wildflowers are particularly plentiful.

The **Uplands Picnic Area** near the Rock City Campground in the southern part of the park on South Gate Road is the trailhead for the **Artist Point/Fossil Ridge Trail**. This easy 1.5-mile round-trip leads through open grassland where flowers are thick during the spring.

Black Point Trail in the northern reaches of the park has one of the most spectacular blooms in the whole Bay Area each spring.

Take Clayton Road exit off I-680 to the town of Clayton. In Clayton turn south on Mitchell Canyon Road and continue to the parking area at the end of the road. Take the Mitchell Canyon Fire Road from the parking area and the lightly used Black Point Trail to the right after about 1.75 miles. Make a loop back to the fire road for a strenuous 4-mile hike.

The roads to **Mt. Hamilton** from both east and west lead through steep terrain where bright patches of wildflowers stand out against the green grasses of spring. From the west take Alum Rock Road off I-680 to CA 130 (Mt. Hamilton Road). This is a very winding road that is best taken slowly as you view the wildflower displays. From the north take Mines Road off I-580 and continue on it until it turns into San Antonio Valley Road.

Both of these roads are narrow and winding, and the best way to see the wildflowers is to make this a day outing where you stop occasionally to view the most outstanding displays. Mt. Hamilton Observatory sits atop the peak and is open occasionally for public visits.

The **McCloud River Preserve** of The Nature Conservancy is more noted for its excellent fly fishing than its wildflower displays, but each is equally good. The preserve is located in an isolated section of the McCloud River east of I-5 where there are good views of Mt. Shasta. To get to the preserve take CA 89 east off I-5 halfway between Dunsmuir and Mt. Shasta City to McCloud. In McCloud head south on Squaw Valley Road at the Shell Station. Follow the signs to Ah-Di-Na campground. Ten miles of this access road is unpaved, narrow and full of potholes, but not steep or slippery.

Continue 1 mile past the campground to the end of the road. Park there and follow the trail for half a mile to the preserve headquarters. They will have information and trail maps. Contact the preserve manager at P.O. Box 409, McCloud, CA 96057; (916) 926-4366 for more information.

San Luis NWR is almost as noted for its wildflowers as its wildlife. Plentiful water and open grasslands make this an excellent drive for wildflower enthusiasts who do not wish to walk any great distances.

The refuge is 10 miles north of Los Banos in the Central Valley. Take North Mercy Springs Road (CR J14) 8 miles to Wolfsen Road. Turn northeast and continue 2 miles to the refuge. You can drive along the top of the levees in search of good displays of wildflowers.

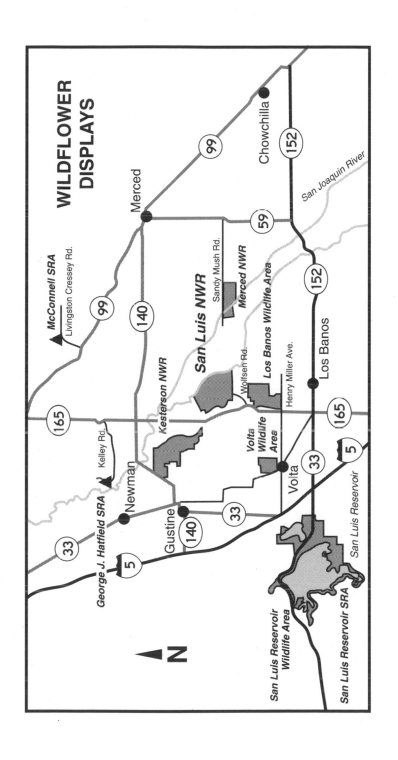

27

Waterfalls in the Sierra and Cascades

While waterfall enthusiasts enjoy the winter waterfalls of the Coast Range, they realize that they are only a preview of the majestic waterfalls that can be seen in the Sierra Nevada and southern Cascades after the snow melts in late spring. Without a doubt the best of these are those located in Yosemite Valley, with some the largest and most famous waterfalls in the United States.

Yosemite Falls, Bridalveil Falls, Nevada Falls, Vernal Falls. All cascade over steep granite cliffs as they flow from hanging valleys high above Yosemite Valley, and after a particularly heavy winter snowpack no other falls in the United States can match them for their beauty and setting.

The problem is they are so famous and popular that you must battle constant crowds along roads and trails as you attempt to get the best views of the falls. There are other falls— not quite so famous, so plentiful or so large as those at Yosemite—but without the crowds, that have spectacular flows in late spring after the snowpack has melted. Some are on well-traveled roads where you can just pull off to the side to view the falls, and others are on more out-of-the-way scenic routes where you must drive for a while to get to the falls.

All, however, are worth the effort for anyone who

wishes to view nature at its fullest power, yet enjoy the peace that many find as they watch the constant flow of water rushing down from great heights.

HOTSPOTS

Yosemite Valley is without doubt the most famous waterfall site in the country. It has tall waterfalls, powerful waterfalls and simply beautiful waterfalls. The only problem is that it is extremely popular. Go early as soon as the snow melts and try to avoid the crowds.

You reach the valley floor by CA 120 from Manteca on CA 99, by CA 140 from Merced on CA 99 or by CA 41 from Fresno on CA 99. Access across Tioga Pass from the east side of the Sierra is closed until June or July each year.

Horsetail Falls near Twin Bridges on U.S. 50 a little over 90 miles east of Sacramento is a double falls that is visible from pullouts after you have passed the small community of Twin Bridges. Check with locals to find out whether the strenuous trail to the bottom of the falls is free of snow.

Feather Falls on Feather River drops 640 feet into a gorge and is one of the most impressive waterfalls in the state outside Yosemite. Although a national recreation trail leads to the falls, there are few crowds. It just isn't that accessible. From Oroville take CA 162 east to Forbestown Road where you turn right. Continue on Forbestown Road to Lumpkin Road. Turn left and continue on this winding road over an arm of Oroville Lake as it becomes La Porte Road. You climb Railroad Grade and pass Sucker Run Road on the right before you come to the parking area for the trailhead. The 3.5-mile-long scenic trail takes you to the falls.

Burney Falls is an impressive 129-foot double waterfall that crashes over basalt cliffs in a forest setting. During the peak of the spring flow well over 100 million gallons of water cascade over the cliffs each day. The falls are in the **McArthur/Burney Falls State Park** which lies northeast of Redding on CA 89, 6 miles north of CA 299.

28

Elk Calves

Herds of elk that seemed endless roamed the grasslands of the Central Valley of California before the arrival of the earliest European settlers. These massive groups wandered over their ranges unimpeded by fence or road. They provided an unending supply of food and hides for the Native Americans who lived in the region, but the elk population was so large that it more than absorbed any loss from hunting.

That wasn't the case after the arrival of the Europeans. With guns and with fences the new settlers quickly decimated the huge population of elk, and this majestic animal almost disappeared from the state. Today small herds are located in protected areas such as Point Reyes National Seashore, Grizzly Island Wildlife Area and Prairie Creek Redwoods SP. These are easily seen much of the year, and one of my favorite times to search them out is soon after the first calves are born.

You are not likely to see large numbers of males with their 5-foot racks at this time, but you will see the young loping along behind their mothers as they browse along the edges of open meadows. They are also fond of grass and will graze in the middle of meadows when there is grass available.

Elk are the largest member of the deer family found in California, and three subspecies reside in the state. Tule elk are the smallest and most numerous of the three forms, and bulls weigh about 500 pounds. Roosevelt elk are the largest of the three forms, and bulls can weigh well over 1,000 pounds. They can be most easily viewed at Prairie Creek State Park north of Eureka. Rocky Mountain elk are the least numerous and are found in numbers only around Lake Shasta in the northern part of the state. Although at a distance elk have a superficial resemblance to mule deer, you are not likely to confuse the two up close because of the dramatic difference in size.

Elk generally give birth to only one calf after about 250 days of gestation and suckle them through the summer. Mating follows the rutting season and takes place in the late summer. See Chapter 43 for where to see rutting elk.

HOTSPOTS

Some of the most accessible herds of Roosevelt elk are found in **Prairie Creek Redwoods SP** along U.S. 101 between Arcata and Orick. Herds can be seen in the open prairie of the park along the highway and in the grass-covered dunes along much of **Gold Bluffs Beach.** Gold Bluffs Beach is reached from U.S. 101 by taking Davison Road west for about 7 miles.

Farther south is **Sinkyone Wilderness SP**, a hard-to-reach wilderness park where the herds are more dispersed. For those who want to see the large Roosevelt elk in a true wilderness setting, this is the place to go. A few narrow and steep roads offer access to this rugged park on the coast. A 17-mile-long trail stretches the length of the park, and you can reach the park by CR 431, which heads west from CA 1 at milepost 90.88 between Leggett and the coast. From the north you take Briceland Road from Redway for 36 miles.

You can search for the herds as you hike along the park trails.

At **Point Reyes National Seashore** are herds of the smaller tule elk. You can see young bulls near the road as you reach the parking area at **Tomales Point Trailhead** at Pierce Ranch in the northern section of the seashore. For views of mothers and calves you need to hike along the trail that extends for about 4 miles past Pierce Ranch.

The seashore lies along CA 1 to the north of Olema and south of Point Reyes Station. To reach the trailhead at Pierce Ranch take Sir Francis Drake Highway from CA 1, and turn right on Pierce Ranch Road. The parking at the trailhead is 9 miles past the junction of Pierce Ranch Road and Sir Francis Drake Highway.

Grizzly Island Wildlife Area also has a herd of tule elk, and they graze on the back side of the duck ponds in the wildlife area. Plans are in the works for a wildlife viewing tower that will rise above the flat countryside. From there you will be able to see the elk herds as they migrate from pasture to pasture during the year. For now, you will have to search for the herds from ground level and view them through binoculars or spotting scopes.

Grizzly Island Wildlife Area is on Suisun Bay, and you can reach it from I-80 near Suisun City by taking CA 12 east past Suisun City to Grizzly Island Road. Turn right on Grizzly Island and continue 14 miles to the game management headquarters. They will furnish you with current information about the herds.

San Luis NWR has another large herd of tule elk, and they can be viewed from the levees as you drive through the refuge.

The refuge is 10 miles north of Los Banos in the Central Valley. Take North Mercy Springs Road (CR J14) 8 miles to Wolfsen Road. Turn northeast and continue 2 miles to the refuge. You can drive along the top of the levees in search of elk.

Owens Valley has one of the largest herds of tule elk in northern California, and you can get directions to it from the Department of Fish and Game. The herds are generally found in the sagebrush country that is part of the Bureau of Land Management lands to the south of Bishop, but a call to (619) 871-1171 will gain you further information. Owens Valley is a large flat valley that lies alongside U.S. 395 to the south of Bishop.

29

May
Shorttakes

DEER WITH FAWN

As you drive along back roads or hike along deserted trails you are likely to see deer with their new fawns. Not that the fawns are easy to see if they know you are near, for their spots are a perfect camouflage when they lie still in the understory of the forest. If you come upon them unexpectedly, though, you can stand and watch them for many minutes. This past year I even had one come up to my truck when I opened the door. It baa'ed at me, until I saw its mother a short distance away. When I shut my door and backed my truck away the mother came to reclaim her lost young.

SKUNK, POSSUM AND RACCOON GALORE

You know it's spring when you drive along country roads and come upon dozens of skunk, possum and raccoon that have been killed by passing cars the night before. As mating activities increase, these animals become at risk as they move across heavily traveled roads. You can see them in a live state if you head out at night with that in mind. Carry a strong flashlight and go to an area with lots of undergrowth and an open water supply and wait. Soon you will hear movement in the brush. As you do, shine your light and you will spot one of the above creatures. The light will hold them for a moment while you get a good look.

For those of us who live in the country, we don't have to go far. Seldom does a night go by that we don't have one or another visit our back steps for a goody. A large male possum even died in our cat bed several years ago.

NESTING BIRDS

This is the time to watch for birds building their nests and then for them feeding their young. Some birds, such as jays and ravens are very noisy as they build their nests and defend their territory, while others are silent and secretive. We had a hummingbird build a nest just outside our basement door several years ago, and we didn't know it until it was already nesting, while the same year a group of ravens built nests in the top of several redwood trees over 100 feet above our heads and we were aware of the activity from the moment they began building.

You will also hear the raucous laughter of Woody Woodpecker, oops, the pileated woodpecker, in many wooded areas this month. You can't miss its call, which was the inspiration for Woody's laugh, or the booming noise it makes as it drills for insects.

30

Breakout: Boggs Lake

Unlike other vernal pools, Boggs Lake is not surrounded by open grassland. Instead it is found amidst a forest of Douglas fir, ponderosa pine, California black oak and madrone. And this is not the only feature that sets Boggs Lake apart from other vernal pools. It is also home to an unusual plant that would be more at home in a southern swamp. Bladderwort has yellow, snapdragonlike blossoms that trap tiny aquatic creatures inside. As deadly as any Venus's flytrap, yellow sheets of bladderwort blossoms cover the surface of the lake and surrounding ponds during the spring, and the carnivorous plants gain extra nutrition from the millions of small aquatic animals that hatch during the same period.

In addition to bladderwort and plants such as downingia, orcutt grass and Indian loveline that are typical of vernal pools, Boggs is home to watershield. This plant lives a life so secretive that its reddish-purple flowers only bloom two successive days during each year. The rest of the time the plant lives beneath the water. The first day of bloom the watershield pushes its blossoms above the water, opens them to receive pollen from other plants then closes them before pulling back beneath the surface of the lake. The next day the blossoms are again pushed to the surface, where they open and disperse their own pollen before disappearing back below the surface.

Boggs Lake lies in a shallow depression in a layer of clay left unfilled by an ancient lava flow. This shallow pool is not fed by springs or streams, but is only a catch basin for the heavy rains that fall in the region during the winter months.

An early pioneer built a sawmill on the shore of the shallow lake just after the Civil War and attempted to deepen it by blasting a large hole in the middle of the lake. The blast created a hole much like a bathtub drain, and all the water in the shallow lake drained into lava caverns below that formed during even more ancient flows than those surrounding the lake. It was only after the hole was filled with nearby impermeable clay that the basin again filled with water.

Today the water recedes as the winter rains stop and the heat of late spring arrives. The brilliant rings of blossoms associated with vernal pools then encircle the slowly shrinking pool.

In addition to the wildflowers, Boggs Lake is noted for its prime bird-watching during nesting season. One hundred forty-two species of birds have been recorded there, including western bluebirds that hover over the open meadows; pileated, downy and hairy woodpeckers that search for insects in the bark of nearby trees; and brown creepers, violet-green swallows and purple martins that nest in the surrounding forests.

The Nature Conservancy owns Boggs Lake, and as always you should check with The Conservancy about visiting any of their preserves. For Boggs Lake contact The Nature Conservancy, 755 Market Street, 3rd Floor, San Francisco, CA 94103; (415) 777-0487 about visiting.

To reach the preserve take CA 29 north from I-80 in Vallejo for 58 miles to CA 175 in Middletown. Take CA

175 northeast 10 miles to the small community of Cobb. Turn left at Bottle Rock Road and go northeast again for 6.5 more miles. Watch for Harrington Flat Road on the right. Turn on it and go 1 mile . The lake and preserve entrance are on the left. Park on the left shoulder of the road near the entrance.

JUNE

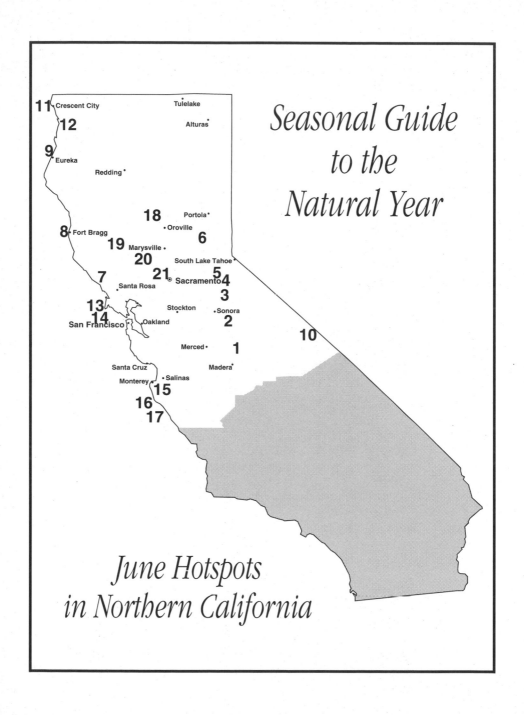

Seasonal Guide
to the
Natural Year

June Hotspots
in Northern California

11 Crescent City   Tulelake
    12   Alturas

9 Eureka
        Redding

                  18   Portola
                          · Oroville
8 · Fort Bragg   6
     19 Marysville ·
       20   South Lake Tahoe
  7   21 · Sacramento 5 4
      · Santa Rosa   3
 13   Stockton   · Sonora
   14   · Oakland   2
San Francisco

                  Merced ·   1
              Madera ·
      Santa Cruz
         Monterey · Salinas
              15
           16
             17

                              10

MAP SITE KEY

1. CA 49: Oakhurst to Mariposa
2. CA 120: Groveland to Crane Flat
3. CA 108: Jamestown to Pinecrest
4. CA 4: Angels Camp to Calaveras Big Trees SP
5. CA 88: Jackson to Carson Pass
6. CA 20: Nevada City to Emigrant Gap
7. Kruse Rhododendron State Reserve
8. Mendocino Coast Botanical Gardens
9. Azalea State Reserve
10. Mono Lake
11. Castle Rock
12. Trinidad State Beach
13. Point Reyes National Seashore
14. Farallon Islands
15. 17-mile Drive
16. Point Lobos State Reserve
17. Hurricane Point
18. Woodson Bridge SRA
19. Colusa/Sacramento River SRA
20. Butte Slough Wildlife Area
21. Bobelaine Ecological Reserve

June Observations

31

Late Wildflowers in the Sierra Foothills

Wildflowers just continue to bloom in Northern California. By June most of the wildflowers of the coast, inland grasslands of the Coast Range and Central Valley have passed their peak, and only stragglers are left to view. That is the time you want to head to the foothills of the Sierra Nevada. After the heat of early summer has hit the Central Valley and the inland areas of the Coast Range the higher reaches of the foothills are just getting warm enough for fields of poppies, lupine, Indian paintbrush and shooting star to brighten the open slopes and pastures alongside the backroads that run through gold country.

These are easily seen by taking leisurely drives through this historic region, with an occasional short hike into larger fields.

From Oakhurst in the south to Grass Valley in the north, CA 49 winds through gold rush country, and several roads head east into the higher reaches of the Sierra Nevada. It is along these that you will see the most luxuriant displays of wildflowers this month.

While the west side of the Sierra is bursting into bloom, the eastern slope also has spots worth visiting. While the sagebrush country of the Great Basin does not have the vibrant displays of the wetter western slope, the canyons and meadows along U.S. 395 as it follows the Walker River do offer some color, as do the road cuts of CA 108 and CA 88 as they head into the high country through Sonora and Carson passes.

HOTSPOTS

These hotspots are primarily drives through the gold rush country from the lower elevations to just below the alpine meadows that bloom later.

The most southern drive is along **CA 49 from Oakhurst to Mariposa**. This is the southernmost part of the gold rush country, and blooms come there about two weeks before those farther north.

North of Yosemite **CA 120 from Groveland to Crane Flat** passes through pine woodlands interspersed with open grasslands and oak forests. Wildflowers bloom in profusion there.

Take **CA 108 from Jamestown to Pinecrest** to head up into the higher foothills where the blooms last later than they do in lower elevations. This route leaves from the heart of the gold rush country and leads from primarily oak grasslands into pine and fir forests.

The next two routes, **CA 4 from Angels Camp to Calaveras Big Trees SP** and **CA 88 from Jackson to Carson Pass** are each beautiful drives that lead through country similar to CA 108, but have slightly later blooms.

The last route, **CA 20 from Nevada City to Emigrant Gap**, is the most northern of the routes and is at the northern end of gold rush country. The blooms here are the latest of all the above routes.

These drives take you through some of the most scenic areas of the Sierra foothills, and you'll pass through numerous historic small towns and near sites of others that disappeared with the gold.

32

Rhododendrons and Wild Azaleas

While the open fields of oak grasslands in the Sierra foothills are filled with blue and gold blossoms, there is also a bright floral display in the redwood forests along the coast. Along creeks and in second growth forests of young redwood, fir, tan oak and bay, blooming wild azaleas and rhododendrons add an unusual display of whites, pinks and reds to the dark and dank forests of the redwood region.

The two large shrubs provide even more vibrant blooms than their cultivated relatives against the dark green backdrop of the dense forests. Both grow in well-watered areas that were cleared by burns earlier in the century. They took root in these clearings as transitional plants that will slowly give way to the encroaching forest. Both like the nitrogen-poor soil found where redwood forests have been cleared.

While these wild shrubs are generally found in isolated small thickets, 317 acres of wild rhododendrons bloom along the edge of a redwood forest at Kruse Rhododendron State Reserve along the Sonoma Coast in Sonoma County. There you can walk among the rhododendrons on several miles of trails. There are short walks for those who only want to explore the edges of the vast thicket of rhododendrons, and longer walks such as the 2.5-mile-long Chinese Gulch/Phillips Gulch Loop for those who want to thoroughly enjoy the experience on foot.

As you head north through redwood country you will find batches of rhododendrons and azaleas throughout the region, but the best sites are in the many redwood parks. There you can contact the rangers to get the specific locations of the shrubs, and walk along quiet trails to reach them. Along with the rhododendrons and azaleas you are also likely to find dogwood and huckleberry blooming.

The farther north you go the later the bloom, and as you reach the Oregon border you may find blooms as late as July in some forests.

HOTSPOTS

These hotspots are specialty gardens and reserves, all found along the coast where the milder climate leads to better blooms. The first is **Kruse Rhododendron State Reserve.** A forest fire destroyed the forests here many years ago and was replaced by thickets of sun-loving rhododendrons. Today the reserve is covered with pink blossoms during the season, and trails—both easy and more strenuous—lead through the blooms.

The reserve sits along CA 1 several miles north of Salt Point SP and about 20 miles north of Jenner.

The **Mendocino Coast Botanical Gardens** were founded in 1961 by a retired nurseryman who purchased 47 acres along CA 1 between Mendocino and Fort Bragg. He cleared underbrush, built trails and planted flowers and shrubs.

In 1992 the Mendocino Coast Recreation and Park District purchased the gardens and opened them to the public. Rhododendrons are only one of the many species of flowering plants that thrive in the lush gardens, but they have the most prominent displays this month.

The gardens are on the ocean side of CA 1, 6 miles north of Mendocino and 2 miles south of Fort Bragg.

Azalea State Reserve is a 30-acre reserve off U.S. 101 that is more noted for its azaleas than rhododendrons, but they are just as splashy. Plus, they are much more fragrant.

Take CA 200 east from U.S. 101 just north of the mouth of the Mad River above Eureka, and follow the signs to the reserve.

33

Mono
Lake

After his first summer in the Sierra John Muir wrote of the Mono Basin, "A country of wonderful contrasts, hot deserts bordered by snow-laden mountains, cinders and ashes scattered on glacier-polished pavement, frost and fire working together in the making of beauty." And the centerpiece of this majestic site was, and continues to be, Mono Lake. One of the oldest lakes in the United States (over seven hundred thousand years old), it covers over 60 square miles and is filled with water so alkaline that Mark Twain wrote, "Its sluggish waters are so strong with alkali that if you dip the most hopelessly soiled garment into them once or twice, and wring it out, it will be found as clean as if it had been through the ablest washerwoman's hands."

For years this large lake—on the east side of the Sierra and across Tioga Pass from Yosemite Valley—was called a dead sea because of its salty water, and in fact few animals can survive there. Those that do survive, however, thrive in astronomical numbers. The food chain in the lake begins with green algae, which turns the lake to a pea soup green during its winter bloom. Brine shrimp and brine fly then feed on this abundant food source and at the height of the summer an estimated four trillion half-inch-long

California gulls feed on the brine shrimp in Mono Lake.

shrimp—or what is left of them—swim in the waters of Mono Lake.

Since 1941, when the City of Los Angeles began diverting water from four of the five major streams that feed Mono Lake, the water level of Mono Lake has dropped over 40 feet and its water has doubled in salinity. This drop seriously threatened the Mono Basin ecosystem, and a court order has restored the stream flow in an attempt to at least maintain the current water level.

Birders were one group that actively supported the fight to restore the water supply to the lake. Nearly three hundred species of birds have been identified in the Mono Basin region, and the health of the lake is crucial to five species of migratory and nesting birds. These are the California gull, Wilson's phalaropes, red-necked phalaropes, eared grebes and snowy plover. All come to gorge on the four trillion brine shrimp in the lake as they nest or stop over on their way to South America.

The shy and seldom seen snowy plover begins the influx of birds in early spring, but they nest in one of the most inaccessible regions of the lake's shore where few venture to see them. After their young are hatched the real invasion begins.

About fifty thousand California gulls—approximately 85 percent of the breeding population of the species—descend upon Mono Lake late each spring to feed along the shore and prepare for nesting. By mid-May they mate, select a nesting site and lay their eggs. These hatch by mid-June, which is a prime time to view the flocks of gulls, and by late July the fledglings will be flying over the water to feed on their own.

By fall all the adults and fledglings will depart for the coast, where the young will live until they return to Mono Lake to breed after they reach maturity at four years of age.

By the time the gulls are most active feeding their hatchlings they are joined on the lake by as many as ninety thousand Wilson's phalaropes. Mono Lake is one of their main stopover sites on their 3,000-mile journey to South America.

Together the California gulls and Wilson's phalaropes provide a spectacular display of birdlife during late spring and early summer. They are joined later in the summer by about 750,000 eared grebe. These cover the lake as far as you can see, and feed, sleep, mate and even build floating nests on the water.

The area around the lake has been protected as the Mono Lake Tufa State Reserve and the Mono Basin National Forest Scenic Area. The forest service has a beautiful and informative visitors' center just north of Lee Vining. There you can obtain information about the best viewing sites along the lake's shore. You can contact the forest service at Mono Basin National Forest Scenic Area Visitors' Center, P.O. Box 429, Lee Vining, CA 93541; (619) 647-6525.

34

Nesting Seabirds

While California gulls leave the Pacific coast and head inland to Mono Lake to nest, millions of other seabirds choose to gather together on rocky islands just off the shore in large nesting colonies. These are generally inaccessible to humans, but many can be seen easily from shore. Others can be viewed from boats after short trips.

Double-breasted, Brandt's and pelagic cormorants, Cassin's auklet, tufted puffin, thin-billed murres and pigeon guillemots are some of the most abundant seabirds that can be viewed during nesting season. Simply drive along the seashore until you come to a rocky islet offshore where the birds are protected from everything but other seabirds.

This is one of the few chances you have to see pelagic seabirds without enduring long boat trips out into the open ocean, which is something many people wish to avoid at all costs.

These nesting colonies frequently number in the millions. The Farallon Islands and Castle Rock off Crescent City are two of the largest colonies of nesting seabirds in the Pacific south of Alaska, and as you get close the noise can be almost deafening. The clamor is just one part of the general excitement of nesting colonies. The hustle and bustle of the nesting sites reminds me of city streets in Chicago or New York as workers rush out of the high-rises at quitting time. Everyone is jostling for a spot on the rocky ledges and whatever level spots there are to be found, and the movement is accompanied by squawks, squeaks and the flapping of wings.

By the time the eggs have hatched all the above sounds are joined by the new sounds of nestlings signaling their hunger to their searching parents.

While some of the hotspots listed below are within easy viewing, most require either strong binoculars or a spotting scope to see the action close-up.

HOTSPOTS

The second largest seabird rookery in California is located on **Castle Rock** off **Point St. George** in Crescent City. Cassin's and rhinoceros auklets are the two most numerous species that nest on the rock, but many other species can also be spotted there. The rock is about half a mile offshore, so you either need a scope or a boat to see the rookery up close. Take 9th Street east from downtown Crescent City until it ends at Pebble Beach. Turn right at the beach and continue along the shoreline to Point St. George.

You can locate excursion boats and boat rentals at Crescent Harbor near downtown.

Trinidad State Beach is the southernmost spot on the Pacific Coast where the tufted puffin can be seen regularly. They are just one of the many species of birds that are attracted to the islets offshore, and this attracts birders from around the world. The best viewing point is at **Elk Head**, which is reached from Stage Coach Road a mile north of the beach. Go past the intersection with Anderson Road for another 200 yards, then turn west on a dirt road. Park your car and follow the marked trails north for about 1 mile to the northernmost point on Elk Head. Two islets lie offshore.

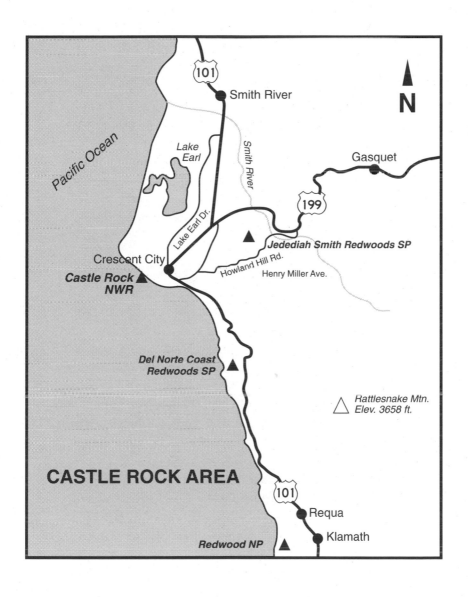

101 Smith River

Pacific Ocean

Lake Earl

Smith River

Gasquet

199

Jedediah Smith Redwoods SP

Lake Earl Dr.

Crescent City

Howland Hill Rd.

Henry Miller Ave.

Castle Rock NWR

Del Norte Coast Redwoods SP

△ Rattlesnake Mtn. Elev. 3658 ft.

CASTLE ROCK AREA

101

Requa

Klamath

Redwood NP

N

For a special treat, near **Trinidad** take a night outing to view the nocturnal, burrow-nesting Leach's storm petrel. Choose an overcast, moonless night and take a strong flashlight to get a view of these birds off Scenic Drive south of Trinidad.

Farther south is the **Point Reyes Lighthouse**. This historical site stands high above the crashing waves below, and you can look down upon the rocks that rise above the wave action to view rookeries of cormorants, murres and guillemots. Follow the signs for Sir Francis Drake Highway from CA 1 just south of Point Reyes Station and continue to the lighthouse. Park and walk down the steps of the long stairway to the lighthouse. Continue past the lighthouse and you will see the rookeries below.

The **Farallon Islands**, which lie in the Pacific Ocean 26 miles out from the Golden Gate, are home to the largest seabird rookery in California and one of the largest south of Alaska. No one is allowed on the islands, but boats can circle around them as birders scope out the nesting colonies of a wide variety of seabirds. Excursion boats (several of which are listed in the appendix) also make naturalist-led trips to the islands during the spring and summer.

While most people take the **Seventeen Mile Drive** south of Monterey to view the coastline, the many golf courses and the beautiful homes that line the fairways, others know that **Point Joe**, **Bird Island** and **Fan Shell Beach** offer some of the best seabird- and shorebird-watching along the entire Pacific Coast. Brandt's cormorants nest on Bird Island, and pelagic and shorebirds abound at the other two. All are easily viewed from pullouts on the drive.

Take Ocean View Drive south from Pacific Grove until it turns into Sunset Drive. The north entrance to the Seventeen Mile Drive is on the right. There is a charge for the drive, which ends in Carmel.

Point Lobos State Reserve, about 3 miles south of Carmel off CA 1, has several large rocks offshore that house rookeries. Get a map at the entrance and continue on the reserve road until it ends at the southern boundary of the reserve. Offshore is Bird Island, where Brandt's cormorants nest on its flat top, pelagic cormorants on its cliffs and western gulls all over. Pigeon guillemots nest on other rocky islets and cliffs nearby.

The last hotspot is **Hurricane Point**, which is located off CA 1 just over 13 miles south of Point Lobos State Reserve. The pullout to the point is on the ocean side of the highway just over 1 mile past Bixby Creek (which is signed). From the pullout you look down at a large rock where several hundred thin-billed murres breed and raise their young.

35

June Shorttakes

CHANGING BEACHES

The beaches all along the coast undergo a change this month. The large, crashing waves of winter become the rolling, low waves that will continue throughout most of the summer, and what were mostly empty beaches begin to fill up with people as the first hot days of summer appear. What we in Northern California see as crowded will surprise many from the south and east, though, for at no time do our beaches become as crowded as those near the major population centers of the south and east. Now is a good time to enjoy sun at the beach, for the fogs that arrive with the heat of mid-summer have yet to appear, and you can actually get some rays as you lie on the sand.

FIRST HOT DAYS OF SUMMER

For most of Northern California the first really hot days don't come until late June. Then the temperatures rise in the high 90s in the Central Valley, and people flock to parks and rivers to enjoy what they will want to leave in the next two months.

For fishermen, this is the time to head for the reservoirs of the Sierra foothills.

36

Breakout:
Yellow-Billed Cuckoo

Each spring yellow-billed cuckoos fly north from South America, where they winter, to the riparian growth along California rivers. There they mate, lay their eggs and raise their young before heading south again in September. During this short stay they forage among the willows for caterpillars (they particularly like the green sphinx-moth caterpillar), grasshoppers, katydids, cicadas and small tree frogs.

The loss of riparian habitat during the past century has been especially hard on the yellow-billed cuckoo in the west. While the population east of the Rockies is large and stable, that to the west has dropped precipitously in this century. They were still quite common as late as 1915, but slowly dwindled as their riparian habitat shrank from about 775,000 acres in California at the turn of the century to about 12,000 acres today.

There were an estimated fifteen thousand mated pairs of yellow-billed cuckoo in California at their peak. Today there are probably fewer than one hundred mated pairs in the state, and these are found in the few remaining remnants of riparian forests along the major rivers in California. In Northern California most are found along the banks of the Sacramento and Feather rivers above Sacramento.

You can hear the distinctive *kuk kuk, kowlp* as you hike through the willow thickets along the banks, or as you canoe slowly down the rivers.

When you hear the cuckoo's call you then begin looking for a nondescript bird about the size and shape of a scrub jay. It is brown above and white below, with a long tail that is black underneath. Its name comes from the long, curved beak with a black upper half and yellow underpart.

The following hotspots are all accessible by car, but if you would like to explore the rivers by canoe you can put in just about anywhere there is a launching facility. Just look for good riparian growth and ask around to find where you can launch a canoe. A word of warning: The Sacramento and Feather rivers are both fast-flowing rivers with levels and flow controlled by upstream dams. If you aren't planning on a one-way trip you should think about heading upriver until you have had enough, then floating back to your starting point.

HOTSPOTS

One of the largest colonies of cuckoos in Northern California is found at **Woodson Bridge SRA** northwest of Chico on the Sacramento River. This 428-acre area sits astride the river, but the undeveloped west side, with only a boat-in campsite, is the best spot to see or hear the cuckoo. The park is 6 miles east of Corning on Sixth Avenue between I-5 and CA 99.

The **Colusa/Sacramento River SRA** is primarily used by fisherman as an RV park and boat launching site, but it includes a large, undisturbed riparian grove along the river. A marked trail leads through this grove, and there you are likely to see or hear the cuckoo during nesting season. The park is near downtown Colusa on the river. Colusa is 9

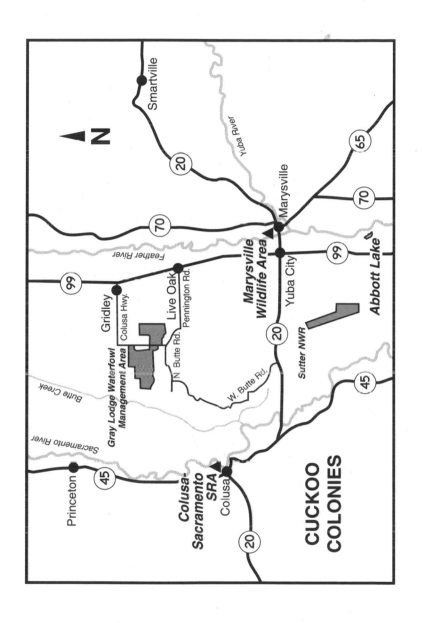

miles east of I-5 on CA 20. Go through town to the end of CA 20 to the recreation area entrance.

Butte Slough Wildlife Area is a little-known refuge that lies at the foot of the Sutter Buttes, and it includes 178 acres of undisturbed riparian habitat. The yellow-billed cuckoo is frequently heard, and occasionally seen, in the thick stands of willow and cottonwood. Take CA 20 west from Yuba City 10 miles to West Butte Road. Turn north and go 3.8 miles to the access road to the wildlife area.

Bobelaine Ecological Reserve is a reserve with a cottonwood forest ecological system and impenetrable thickets. This Audubon reserve is open to the public and has well-maintained trails that lead through the thickets and forests. There are also several marked observation points where birding is excellent. Take Laurel east from CA 99 about 15 miles south of Marysville/Yuba City. The road dead-ends at the preserve entrance.

JULY

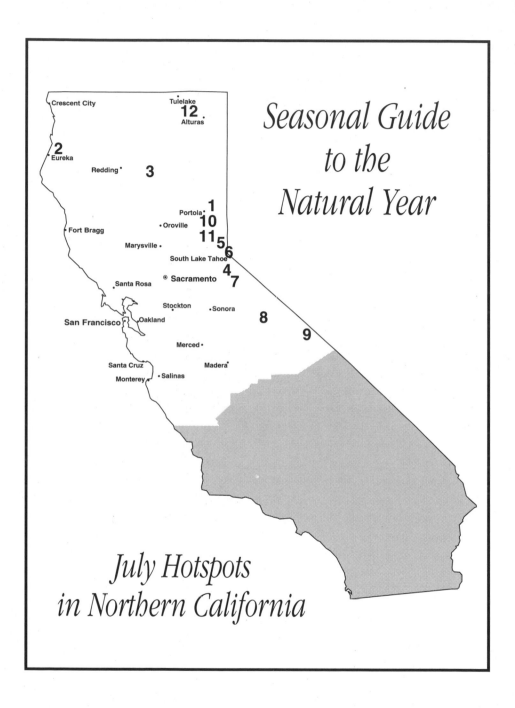

Seasonal Guide to the Natural Year

Crescent City

Tulelake
12
Alturas

2
Eureka

Redding

3

Portola
1
Oroville
10
Fort Bragg
11 5
6
Marysville
South Lake Tahoe
4
Santa Rosa
7
Sacramento

Stockton
Sonora
San Francisco
Oakland
8
9
Merced

Santa Cruz
Madera
Monterey
Salinas

*July Hotspots
in Northern California*

MAP SITE KEY

1. Plumas-Eureka SP
2. Lake Earl Wildlife Area
3. Lassen Volcanic NP
4. Desolation Wilderness
5. Sugar Pine SP
6. D. L. Bliss/Emerald Bay SP
7. Carson Pass Area
8. Yosemite NP
9. Devils Postpile National Monument
10. Bassett's Station and San Francisco State University Sierra Nevada Field Campus
11. Donner Pass and Donner Memorial SP
12. Tule Lake NWR

July Observations

37

Beaver Ponds

With the possible exception of precious metals such as gold and silver, beavers were more responsible for westward expansion in the United States than any other single thing. The pelts of these large rodents—they are the largest rodent in North America at up to 50 pounds—were highly prized during the late 1700s and early 1800s, and trappers headed west as they decimated the eastern beaver population. While beavers lived in almost every section of the country, they were more abundant in the Pacific Northwest than in any other.

The demand for pelts was unceasing for several decades and the beaver was trapped almost to extinction. As the demand dropped and trapping ceased, the rodent began its climb back from the brink and now can be found along quiet waterways throughout its former territory. This is particularly true in California, where beavers are found throughout the northern section of the state except along the coast. Beavers are even considered a pest by many farmers and ranchers now, for they frequently disrupt the flow of water as they build dams to create small ponds. Today you can see the industrious animal at work in many state parks and along waterways in the Sacramento/San Joaquin Delta.

Beaver dams dot meadows of the High Sierra.

The beaver prefers quiet ponds surrounded by deciduous trees such as aspen, birch, alder and willow. They build dome-shaped lodges with an entrance underwater in the midst of these ponds. If there is no pond, beavers build dams along slow-moving streams to create one. Occasionally, but not frequently, beavers will live along large rivers and fast-flowing canals, where they burrow into the soft banks to make their lodges.

Wherever it lives, the beaver alters the environment more than any animal except humans. Their ponds create new habitat for aquatic animals where none existed, and they expand openings in forests where both sun-loving wildlife and plants can survive where they couldn't previously. Even most of the pocket meadows one frequently crosses along High Sierra streams are filled-in, abandoned beaver ponds.

In the Sacramento/San Joaquin Delta, with its vast network of levees, beavers thrive in both the backwaters of the sloughs and in burrows in the soft levees along the main waterways.

Beavers are particularly active during summer after the birth of their kits. By July the kits are old enough to move outside their lodges for short periods, and you can occasionally spot them in the clear waters of beaver ponds in the upper Sacramento Valley, the foothills of the Sierra Nevada and in the high country of the Sierra Nevada, Cascade and Siskiyou ranges. You are most likely to see these industrious creatures at dawn and dusk as they gather food among the young trees that surround their ponds.

Beavers move as the supply of young trees, whose inner bark is a food source, gives out. They stay in the same general area, though, as they build another dam or find another shallow pond in which to build their lodge. The deserted ponds slowly fill with debris and form a small pocket meadow that is eventually overgrown by the encroaching forest.

HOTSPOTS

Any trek into the high country of the mountains of Northern California is likely to lead you to meadows with beaver ponds. You can also see them along many riparian sites near the major rivers of the region, but there is one spot where you can't miss seeing working beaver ponds.

Plumas-Eureka SP lies north of Lake Tahoe off CA 89 near the restored mining community of Johnsville. The park and surrounding national forest land include a wide range of ecological communities. These range from mountain peaks over 6,000 feet high, high mountain lakes, alpinelike meadows, streamside habitats and a large meadow where beaver have been in residence for decades. There you can walk along trails that lead you into the middle of the beaver ponds. Dams, lodges, vast areas of deforested meadows and ponds full of active beavers all make this one of the prime spots in California to see beavers at work.

Take CA 89 north just over 45 miles from Truckee to Graeagle. At Graeagle turn west on Johnsville-Graeagle Road (CR A14) and continue for 5 miles to Johnsville and the park headquarters.

Another area where you are almost assured of seeing active beavers is the **Lake Earl Wildlife Area**. The lake lies in the floodplain of the Smith River just north of Crescent City. The wildlife area begins at the coast and includes two connected lakes, ancient sand dunes, seasonal wetlands and upland fields and forests of fir and Sitka spruce. It is along the edge of the forests that you will find both beaver and river otter activity.

From Crescent City take Lake Earl Drive north to Old Mill Road. Turn left on Old Mill and continue for 1.5 miles to the wildlife area headquarters.

38

Alpine Flowers

California's seven-month spring continues into July as the high alpine meadows of the Sierra Nevada burst forth into full bloom. At elevations of 6,000 feet and above the growing season is short and the plants that survive there must take full advantage of every opportunity. The mountain snowpack buries alpine meadows beneath 20, 30, or even 40 feet of snow during normal years, and it is only after that snowpack has melted that the flowers can begin their rapid growth toward bloom.

The meadows tend to be soggy or at least moist and are found near lakes, along streams and below snowbanks that stay late into the summer. Large plants are missing from the plant communities found in the meadows, and only an occasional shrub willow rises above the sedges and forbs that dominate the landscape.

As the snow melts and the water level recedes enough for the flowers to germinate, alpine meadows become veritable artist's palettes of color. Alpine goldenrod, aster, cinquefoil, saxifrage, paintbrush, gentian, shooting star and buttercup provide hues of red, pink, yellow and blue that are spattered across the green meadows. Some of the stands are as much as a foot tall, but most alpine wildflowers are low-lying plants that can withstand the windy, harsh environment of the alpine climate.

Alpine meadows in the Sierra are sunnier and warmer than those in most mountain ranges in the United States, and this makes the wildflower displays even more profuse than those found in most other ranges. They are also drier in general than other mountain ranges during the summer, and the landscape surrounding the meadows has a more desertlike appearance. The displays are even more noticeable as a result.

Plants begin to grow and bloom first on the south-facing slopes above the meadows, followed by open meadows where the snow may melt early but the soil remains so cold and damp that few plants can germinate. The north- and east-facing slopes are the last to lose their snowpack and the last to break out in wildflower bloom. The timing of the bloom depends upon the melt of the snowpack, and that varies tremendously each year. In some years the south-facing slopes may be free of snow by late May and have a bloom by early June. In others they may not be free of snow until well into July and not have the first bloom until late July. In those years there will be blooms in the meadows as late as September, just in time for the winter snows to come again. In normal years the peak of the alpine meadow blooms is mid-July.

While my favorite way to view alpine meadows in full bloom is to hike into isolated areas where I can view meadows from above, there are plenty of areas where the meadows can be seen from the road, or by a short walk.

HOTSPOTS
Lassen Volcanic NP is in the southern end of the Cascade Mountains, which are justly noted for their alpine flowers farther north in Oregon and Washington. Although the Lassen region is slightly lower in elevation than the Cascades farther north, it is still a wildflower wonderland

after the snow melts. Elevations below 6,500 feet have snow four to five months a year, while those up to 8,000 feet are under as much as 20 feet of snow for seven months.

The short growing season between the snowmelt and the first fall snows, plus the abundant ground water, make the alpine meadows in the park colorful gardens of reds, blues and yellows during midsummer.

Most of the park is in wilderness backcountry, where you can hike to wildflower meadows from many trailheads. The main road through the park is the 34 miles of CA 89 that runs from the south entrance to the north on a circuitous route. Along the road are many pullouts and meadows where you can see wildflower displays.

The park can be reached via CA 36 from Red Bluff or CA 44 from Redding.

Desolation Wilderness, which lies in the High Sierra to the west of Lake Tahoe, is one of the most visited wilderness areas in California, and a visit there during the peak wildflower bloom shows why the 63,475-acre area is so popular. The **Pacific Crest Trail** crosses the wilderness north to south and the **Tahoe Rim Trail** will lead through portions of it when completed.

You can enter the wilderness from a number of trailheads, and access is limited. You can reserve a pass at the El Dorado National Forest District Headquarters in Camino. Call (916) 644-6048 for more information about reservations and the best locales for wildflowers.

One access to Desolation Wilderness is **Sugar Pine SP**, which lies along the side of Lake Tahoe off CA 89. For those who do not wish to extend themselves too much, several hikes within this delightful park lead to wildflower-filled meadows.

The park entrance is off CA 89 25 miles south of I-80. It is 10 miles past Tahoe City.

About 10 miles farther south along CA 89 is **D.L. Bliss/Emerald Bay SP**. Desolation Wilderness is also accessible from this park, but you need go no farther than the short trails within the park to find beautiful displays of alpine flowers.

The park entrance is off CA 89 about 44 miles south of I-80, or 19 miles south of Tahoe City.

For a true alpine wildflower drive you can't beat, take the drive along CA 88 from its junction with CA 89 to **Carson Pass** and **Silver Lake**. This drive takes you along the Carson River and across long alpine meadows before ascending the steep eastern slope of the Sierra to Carson Pass. All along the way you will see colorful displays of wildflowers.

From the U.S. Forest Service visitors' center at Carson Pass a trail leads south into the **Mokelumne Wilderness Area**. Frog Lake is about .5 mile in along the trail, and from there the trail leads to Winnemucca and Round Top lakes. All of these lakes sit in the shadow of 10,000-foot Round Top peak.

The area between Frog and Round Top lakes has been designated as the **Round Top Botanical Area** by the USFS and has an outstanding variety of wildflowers. The hike is relatively easy, and many Native Plant and Sierra Club groups make day hikes into the area to view the wildflowers.

The junction of CA 89 and 88 is 11 miles south of U.S. 50 near Lake Tahoe.

The ultimate alpine wildflower trip in California is to **Tuolumne Meadows** in **Yosemite NP**. These High Sierra meadows are covered with snow for as much as eight months of the year, and their broad, flat landscape offers little drainage for the melting snow. As the cold waters seep into the ground the heat from the summer sun encourages large patches of alpine wildflowers to flourish.

You reach Tuolumne Meadows on CA 120 which crosses the Sierra Nevada at Tioga Pass. Yosemite Valley is to the west of the pass and Mono Lake is to the east.

Farther south and on the east side of the Sierra is **Devils Postpile National Monument**. The monument was set aside to give visitors access to a geological phenomenon, columnar-jointed lava, but wildflowers in the surrounding alpine meadows are a great draw each year. Shuttle buses service the monument from the town of Mammoth Lakes from early June to Labor Day each summer. There are also miles of hiking trails in and around the monument that lead through wildflower displays.

39

Hummingbirds

Summertime is hummingbird time, and throughout Northern California you can see a variety of these tiny birds as they scurry from bush to bush searching for nectar-laden flowers. There they hover in midair as they feed.

On lazy summer afternoons when little is moving, less than energetic bird-watchers can have it both ways. They can relax in the shade with a cool drink while keeping an eye and ear out for these smallest of birds. Your ears may pick up their presence before your eyes do, for not only do they whir through the air with a distinctive sound, males constantly chatter as they fight for territory.

Hummingbirds are the most colorful species of birds found in North America, with iridescent green, blue and red feathers arrayed in colorful motifs, but it is difficult to observe these bright colors as the birds hurry back and forth gathering nectar to sustain their high metabolism. With wingspeeds of 50 to 75 beats per second, a pulse rate of 615 beats per minute and a body temperature of 104 degrees Fahrenheit, hummers can't afford to sit still for long.

If you select a site where hummers congregate, such as Sardine Lake or Bassett's Station in the Sierra Nevada, you can get a much closer look at their brilliant colors. As you sit near feeders or hummingbird-attracting flowers you can enjoy a good rest while you bird-watch.

Seven species of hummingbirds are found in Northern California, and six of them breed here. These range in size from the calliope, which is about 2 3/4 inches long, to the Anna's, which can reach 4 inches in length. The others are the black-chinned, Costa's, broad-tailed, rufous and Allen's.

Of these, the ones most commonly seen in the Sierra during midsummer are the calliope, Anna's, black-chinned, rufous and broad-tailed.

Other than in the high country of the Sierra hummers are seen in profusion along the coast, where flowers bloom almost year round. This is the preferred habitat of the Allen's.

HOTSPOTS

You will encounter hummingbirds throughout the High Sierra in midsummer, but are more likely to see them around large meadows where summer blossoms are at their peak.

Five miles east of Sierra City on CA 49 is **Bassett's Station**. This rustic stop with gas station, motel and general store is an excellent place to take a break. They have a large front porch with plenty of hummingbird feeders. Buy a cold drink and sit for a while. You will see several species of hummers assault the feeders.

Head north on Gold Lake Road at Bassett's and continue for 1.5 miles. Watch for the signs to **Deer Lake Trail** and **Sardine Lake**. Follow the dirt road a short distance to the compound at Sardine Lake. The lake boasts a restaurant, lodge, lakeside cabins, fishing, boating, hiking and fine birding. Stop here for an afternoon, an overnight or a week and you will see plenty of hummers.

If you choose not to head for Sardine Lake from Bassett's you may want to continue another mile along CA 49 to the **Sierra Nevada Field Campus of San Francisco State University**. This is a birder's mecca during the

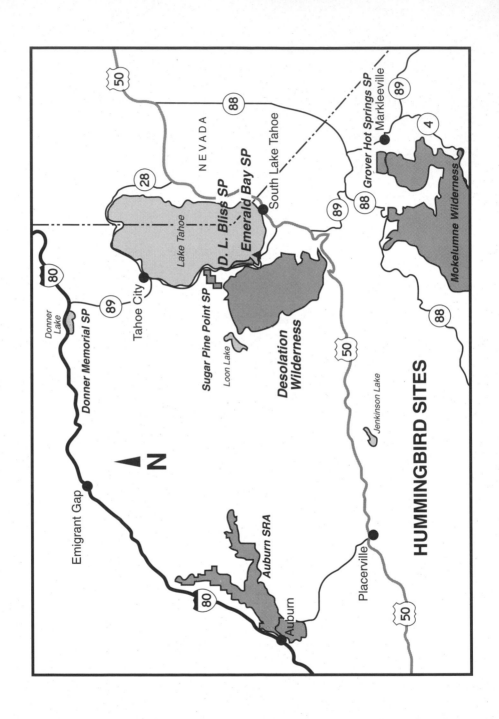

HUMMINGBIRD SITES

summer. Not only are there plenty of birds, the university also offers a number of popular ornithology classes. A catalog of these courses is available from San Francisco State University.

Closer to the highly traveled I-80 is **Donner Memorial SP**. This park sits on the west end of Donner Lake, and trails lead to streamside meadows where hummingbirds congregate to feed on the vast stands of wildflowers.

Take the CA 89 exit south off I-80 to Tahoe City and take a right immediately to the park entrance.

D.L. Bliss/Emerald Bay SP is another wildflower site where hummers collect nectar. Short trails within the park allow you to find beautiful displays. The park entrance is off CA 89 about 44 miles south of I-80, or 19 miles south of Tahoe City.

Hummingbirds congregate at almost all the high meadows in **Yosemite NP** during wildflower bloom. You can get information about the best spots at the visitors' center in Yosemite Valley.

You reach the valley floor by CA 120 from Manteca on CA 99, by CA 140 from Merced on CA 99 or CA 41 from Fresno on CA 99. Access across Tioga Pass on CA 120 from the east side of the Sierra is closed until June or July each year.

40

Canoeing Tule Lake National Wildlife Refuge

During the winter the waters of Tule Lake NWR are either covered with huge flocks of ducks and geese or frozen solid enough to walk on. By midsummer the vast flocks of waterfowl have left for the north, although a tremendous number of other birds stay on to nest and raise their young. It is then that the shallow waterways are open for canoeing the trails established by the refuge managers.

Although this refuge should not be missed during the fall and winter when huge numbers of migrating birds congregate here to feed and rest, summer is not exactly a bust. Many ducks and shorebirds nest here, and during midsummer you can see their fledglings getting ready for the fall migration. The grebe carry their young around on their backs, even as they dive beneath the surface, until they are old enough to dive for themselves.

An auto tour route takes you along several dikes that provide excellent vantage points, but a canoe trip through the refuge takes you among the thousands of birds where you hear, see and feel their presence.

Between July and September you can launch your canoe for a two- or three-hour trip.

Tule Lake NWR includes almost 40,000 acres of open

water, marshes, uplands and croplands, is a feeding site for the largest wintering population of bald eagles in the lower forty-eight states (see Chapter 2) and is a stopover for 85 to 90 percent of all waterfowl in the western United States.

The canoe trail begins along Lost River off East-West Road between the town of Tulelake and the refuge head-quarters and visitors' center. You should head for the visitors' center first, where you can get a trail map, and then head back toward Tulelake. Turn south on the first road past Lost River and continue to the end to the launch site. The visitors' center is located on Hill Road .5 mile south of East-West Road, which dead-ends into Hill.

41

July
Shorttakes

BLUE FLOWERS OF CHICORY

By this time most of the blooms that have covered fields and hillsides of Northern California since March have disappeared, but a lonely straggler beats the odds and can be seen in disturbed ground along roadways. The bright blue blooms of wild chicory open atop tall stalks this month and give some color to the roadside.

SUMMER HEAT WAVES

Residents of the Central Valley don't relish the coming of midsummer, when it is not unusual for temperatures to rise above 100. When a heat wave hits the valley and stays for days or weeks the residents head for the hills—the hills of the Sierra, where the higher elevations moderate the heat that blankets the lower valley. Those who don't head for the hills head for the ocean. There they find a cool respite for, when the temperatures rise for an extended period in the valley, the fog rolls in off the ocean to cover the coastline.

42

Breakout:
Water Ouzel

John Muir called the water ouzel "the hummingbird of the Sierra," and wrote one of the best birding stories ever about his experiences with this delightful bird. Better known as American dippers, ouzels spend their entire lives in or near the water.

They look like wrens on steroids as they bob up and down in their search for aquatic insects and small fish along the bottom of fast-flowing streams. They even dive for food in the deeper pools of streams where they walk submerged along the bottom.

Although you may catch an ouzel in flight over a stream, you will seldom see one flying over dry land, even for short distances. They live and die by the water.

Water ouzels are very distinctive with their dark feathers, large wrenlike bodies with stubby tails and unmistakable bobbing motion. They never appear motionless as they flit from one section of the stream to another and bob at the knees as they peck for food.

While they are distinctive, they are also seldom seen by the casual observer. Few people seem to look along streams for birds, and many miss the ouzel as a result. Those who do scan the banks and rocks of fast-flowing mountain streams, however, can frequently enjoy for hours at a time one of the most fascinating birds of America.

During early summer you will see ouzels flitting from the streambed to an overhang in the bank or into a rock crevice above the stream. If you look closely you will spot a nest. Even at birth the baby ouzels are not far from water, and they will spend the rest of their lives following the flow of mountain streams.

During summer, and anytime after the snow melts and the streams are free of ice, you will find ouzels along high mountain streams in Northern California. Some of the best places to spot ouzels are also some of the most scenic spots in the state. Yosemite NP, Lake Tahoe Basin and Lassen Volcanic NP are some of the best.

HOTSPOTS

Muir wrote about his experiences with the water ouzel in **Yosemite NP,** and the backcountry streams of the park's wilderness areas are still one of the prime spots to see this "hummingbird of the Sierra."

Ask at the park visitors' center for the best spots to watch for the ouzel.

You reach the valley floor by CA 120 from Manteca on CA 99, by CA 140 from Merced on CA 99 or CA 41 from Fresno on CA 99. Access across Tioga Pass on CA 120 from the east side of the Sierra is closed until June or July each year.

Other good spots to see the water ouzel are the streams that feed into Lake Tahoe. Any of the state parks around the lake, such as **D.L. Bliss/Emerald Bay SP** and **Sugar Pine**, have trails that lead along streams where the ouzel may be seen. (See Chapter 32 for directions to both.)

One place where the ouzel is found around a lake rather than along streams is at **Manzanita Lake** in **Lassen Volcanic NP**. Manzanita is near the north entrance to the park, which is reached from I-5 near Redding on CA 44.

AUGUST

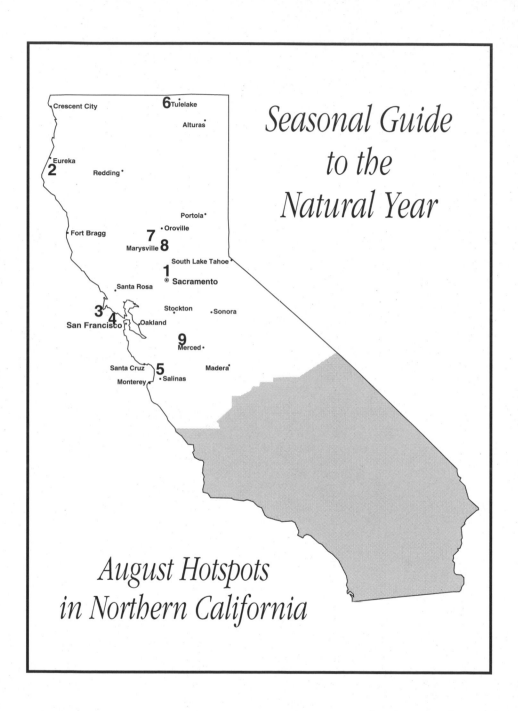

Seasonal Guide to the Natural Year

August Hotspots in Northern California

MAP SITE KEY

1. American River Parkway
2. Humboldt Bay NWR
3. Tomales Bay
4. Bolinas Lagoon
5. Elkhorn Slough National Estuarine Research Reserve
6. Upper Klamath NWR
7. Sacramento NWR Complex
8. Gray Lodge Wildlife Area
9. San Joaquin Valley NWR Complex

August Observations

43

Summer Waterfalls in Gold Country

Waterfalls are to view, not to play in. That is, unless you are exploring the side canyons where tributaries of the major river systems of the Sierra Nevada drop over granite outcroppings as they enter the river gorges.

In spring after the snowpack above melts these falls are roaring cascades of frigid water that no sensible person would ever consider playing in or around. By late summer the volume of water dropping over the falls decreases dramatically, and its temperature rises to only stimulating. The air temperature is near or over 100 degrees in the sun-filled canyons of the gold rush country by then, and a dip into pools beneath cool falls is more than welcome to those who happen upon them as they hike in the canyons.

Some like these falls so much they don't bother exploring the side canyons for new ones, but head straight for ones they know about to enjoy the bracing showers as they play in the water beneath the falls on hot summer days.

Trails lead along the slopes above most of the rivers between Mariposa to the south and Nevada City to the north, and these are kept in good condition by the many gold miners who explore the rivers and their tributaries for what would have been considered minute amounts of the precious

Pools beneath summer waterfalls are great places to cool off in the hot weather of summer.

metal by miners in the mid-1800s. Today's miners are in it more for the fun and adventure than the wealth and are often pleased when they just get color as they pan along the river and stream beds.

That gold remains is not surprising, since this is the heart of the gold rush country. What is surprising is that so little remains of many of the gold mining camps that sprang up literally overnight along the bars of gravel and sand deposits where gold was most plentiful. Today you may see the remains of a fireplace or a corner of a foundation, but little else.

While you can often hike in a mile or so to a waterfall these days and not encounter a soul, in the 1860s and 1870s there were camps with as many as three or four thousand residents that extended up the slopes above rivers near particularly rich deposits.

There are a number of major drainage rivers on the western slope of the Sierra Nevada, including the Stanislaus, Mokelumne, San Joaquin, Tuolumne, American and Yuba rivers. All of these rise dramatically during spring runoff and occasionally rise high enough to do major damage to nearby towns.

The three forks of the American River all feed into Folsom Reservoir. This large reservoir, which is administered by the U.S. Army Corps of Engineers, lies upstream from Sacramento and serves as a flood control and hydroelectric project. The river system provides drainage for the Sierra Nevada between U.S. 50 and I-80 and during the spring runoff often moves house-sized boulders down stream with its furious rush to the ocean.

There are few indications of this force by late summer, however, as many of the tributaries dry up completely, and the main forks of the river are slow-moving streams with occasional large, deep pools.

The north and middle forks are accessible from I-80 above Auburn, and the south fork from U.S. 50 above Placerville. I know the north and middle forks better than the south, and all the falls listed below are along those. You can search for your own falls along the tributaries of the other river systems in gold rush country.

HOTSPOTS

These falls are all short hikes off dirt roads that traverse the canyons of the American River. The first,

Codfish Falls, is an easy hike of about a half mile along Codfish Creek off Ponderosa Way. From Weimar on I-80 east of Auburn take Ponderosa Way for just over 3 miles to a bridge across the North Fork of the American River. About 2 miles of the road are paved, and the rest is maintained gravel. Park along the side of the road before the bridge and head downriver (southwest) on a well-used trail to Codfish Creek. Head upstream until you reach the falls.

Two falls are accessible off Yankee Jim Road out of Colfax off I-80. Take the Canyon Way exit off I-80 before you reach Colfax, and then a right on Canyon Way. Yankee Jim Road is on the right after about a mile. Yankee Jim Road crosses the North Fork of the American after about 3 miles (2 of dirt). You can park on the side of the road just after you cross a unique swinging bridge (the only one of its kind in California). The Indian Creek Trail heads upriver for a little over 1.5 miles to Indian Creek. Take a right and follow the creek upstream to **Indian Creek Falls**. You will cross Shirttail Creek, a small seasonal stream, and Salvation Ravine before you reach Indian Creek.

If you continue on Yankee Jim Road about another .5 mile you will cross Devil's Canyon on the right. Park along the road and hike less than a quarter mile upstream to **Devil's Falls**.

For a short hike to falls on the North Fork of the American River take the Colfax-Iowa Hill Road out of Colfax for about 2 miles. As the road crosses the north fork the Mineral Bar Campground is on the left. Park there, or on the right side of the road, and follow the trail along the east side of the river downstream. You will encounter **Chamberlain Falls** after about 1.5 miles of easy hiking.

44

Migrating Warblers

Warblers seem little more than LBBs (Little Bitty Birds) as they hustle among trees and shrubs in their search for food during their migration south. These small, nondescript birds can be about in great numbers without causing a ruckus or attracting the attention of those not searching for them.

Only 5 inches long at the most (except for the yellow-breasted chat which reaches 7 inches), and generally grayish in color, warblers are easily missed. Even those with brighter markings are overlooked as they hide among the green foliage of summer. Yet when viewed close-up through binoculars warblers are some of the prettiest birds around. Townsend's and hermit warblers both have plenty of yellow contrasting with black, while the MacGillivray's is more muted in its markings.

Whatever warblers you find in your search through riparian vegetation or open woodlands you will have to look carefully to identify them. If you're a casual birder like I am, you will be satisfied with locating lovely small birds as they scrutinize each crack and crevice of a tree in search of small insects. Although it often appears that individual warblers seldom find prey there are so many that they are the scourge of insects and very beneficial to gardens and plants.

There have been fifty-three species of warblers sighted in the West, although you are unlikely to see more than a dozen in any one location. Even that many makes it imperative that you take along a bird identification guide if you are interested in identifying each warbler you see and developing a list of the birds you spot.

Binoculars are also a necessity, and even with a good pair be prepared to be frustrated in many of your efforts since only small differences in markings distinguish many types of the birds.

HOTSPOTS

Warblers are found throughout Northern California as they make their southerly migration in the late summer and early fall, but the **American River Parkway** in Sacramento is an ideal spot to look for them. This 27-mile-long parkway along the American River from Nimbus Dam to the confluence of the American and Sacramento rivers near Old Sacramento has extensive riparian growth that ranges from thick stands of willow and cottonwood to open oak groves. It also offers dirt hiking and paved biking trails that extend the entire distance.

You can begin a birding excursion anywhere along the parkway, but a good place to start is at the **Effie Yeaw Nature Center** in **Ancil Hoffman Park**. The visitors' center there has excellent displays on the riparian habitat, and docents can often point you to the best spots to find the birds you wish to see.

From U.S. 50 take Watt Avenue north to Fair Oaks Boulevard. Turn right on Fair Oaks and continue for several miles to Van Alstine Avenue in Carmichael. Take another right and continue to California Avenue, where you turn left. Continue one block to Tarshes Drive, where you turn right and head into the park. Follow the signs to the nature center.

There are over a dozen access points to the parkway, and you can get a map of the parkway and its regional parks at the nature center.

45

Sharks and Rays

Sharks and rays generally are seen only when someone hauls them aboard a fishing vessel, but each summer you can view leopard sharks, smoothhound sharks and bat rays at selected spots in Northern California as they enter shallow waters of sloughs and lagoons to spawn and feed on the fish and crab.

These are not giants and are very unlike the popularized great white sharks that immediately come to mind when the word "shark" is mentioned. Instead they are relatively small, gentle creatures that cruise along the bottom of shallow waters in search of food and spawning sites.

The best way to view these is by canoe or kayak as you slowly skim over clear, shallow waters. When you see a number of sharks or rays you can stop paddling and let your momentum carry you quietly overhead. The sharks and rays will not scatter unless you make unnecessary noises with your paddles, or someone stomps their feet against the bottom of the canoe.

HOTSPOTS

Humboldt Bay is a long (about 10 miles in length), shallow bay with a high concentration of wildlife. Waterfowl and shorebirds are found here in abundance year-round. Heavy storms hit the bay each winter and move the undeveloped dunes of the 4.5-mile-long south spit over roads and fences. There are over 9 miles of beach around the bay shores, but sharks and rays are best seen from the water. Kayaks and canoes can be launched from the ramp at the jetty.

Tomales Bay lies to the east of the northern section of the **Point Reyes National Seashore** and directly over the San Andreas Fault. It is separated from the Bolinas Lagoon to the south by a small isthmus that is temporarily filled-in marshland. The bay is a long, relatively shallow inlet that is a breeding ground for a number of open ocean fish, including several species of sharks and rays. These include the great white shark. Tomales is not a great viewing spot for spawning sharks and rays since its waters are generally murky and waves keep small craft from gliding quietly over the shallows where the viewing is best. The chance to see great white sharks is tempting to some, however, and there are several launching ramps along the east side of the bay along CA 1.

The northern portion of **Bolinas Lagoon** is a wildlife preserve with a large population of herons and egrets. Those that nest in nearby Audubon Canyon Ranch come to the mudflats around the lagoon to feed. The lagoon separates the southern tip of the Point Reyes Peninsula from the mainland, and the San Andreas Fault runs directly beneath it. There are a number of launch sites along CA 1 north of Stinson Beach on the east side of the lagoon, and the shallow waters are easily rowed by canoe, kayak or boat. Bolinas Lagoon is much more protected, therefore calmer, than the larger and deeper Tomales Bay to the north, and that makes it much easier to spot sharks and rays as they swim along the bottom.

Elkhorn Slough National Estuarine Research Reserve is located inland from Monterey Bay, and is

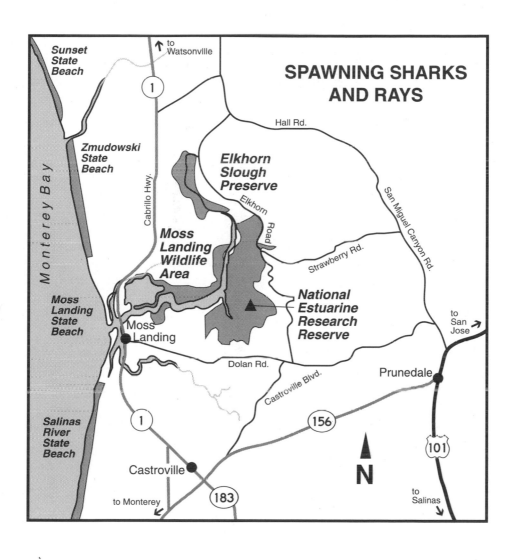

SPAWNING SHARKS AND RAYS

Monterey Bay

Sunset State Beach

Zmudowski State Beach

Moss Landing State Beach

Salinas River State Beach

to Watsonville

1

Hall Rd.

Cabrillo Hwy.

Elkhorn Slough Preserve

Elkhorn Road

Moss Landing Wildlife Area

San Miguel Canyon Rd.

Strawberry Rd.

National Estuarine Research Reserve

to San Jose

Moss Landing

Dolan Rd.

Prunedale

Castroville Blvd.

1

156

101

to Salinas

N

Castroville

to Monterey

183

operated by the California Department of Fish and Game under an agreement with the Division of Marine and Estuarine Management of the National Oceanic and Atmospheric Administration. The Nature Conservancy has a preserve that adjoins the research reserve. Together the two form an outstanding wetlands preserve where many forms of rare and endangered species live. Sharks and rays enter the slough this month to spawn and may be seen along many of the wood walkways that wind through the wetlands.

Take CA 1 south from Watsonville to Dolan Road just before you reach Moss Landing. Take a left at Dolan and continue 3.5 miles to Elkhorn Road. Turn left onto Elkhorn and go another 2.5 miles to the visitors' center.

46

Meteor Showers

Each August near mid-month the night skies are filled with fireworks, as particles that vary from the size of sand grains to that of small pebbles dive through the earth's upper atmosphere. As these particles reach the thicker layers of the atmosphere around 50 to 80 miles up they turn to brightly burning streaks of fire that whisk across the night sky on a regular basis.

These shooting stars, as they are commonly called, are from comet Swift-Tuttle, a ball of ice that loops around the sun every 130 years. Each time the comet draws near the sun it melts a little, leaving a trail of tarlike material in its wake. As the Earth flies through the comet's path each year in August, the particles bombard the atmosphere in what is known as the Perseid meteor showers, since they appear to originate from the constellation Perseus in the northeastern section of the night sky.

During even the worst years as many as five to ten meteors an hour brighten the sky, and during the best as many as two per minute can be seen. On those nights you can get a crick in your neck twisting back and forth attempting to pick up all the meteors shooting out of the starry background.

There is no set way to watch for meteorites, which meteors are called after they enter the atmosphere. They are best seen away from the bright lights of the city where you can have an unobstructed view of the night skies. Beyond that, people have their own favorite ways to watch. Some pick out a small section of sky and simply watch it for an extended period. Others keep up a moving scan of the northern portion of the sky, with their eyes constantly on the move. Still others seem not to have any method, but alternately scan the sky and stare intently at a small section.

Whichever method you use you will still pick up shooting streaks out of the corner of your eye. Some of these are short-lived and are easily missed, while others seem to streak from horizon to horizon, leaving behind a glowing tail. Some even come so close that you can hear a muted explosion as they become superheated and explode low in the atmosphere below the normal 50 to 80 miles. All travel through the atmosphere at a mind-boggling 40 miles per second, so it is no wonder they generally burn before they reach the Earth's surface. Only those the size of large rocks even have a chance.

HOTSPOTS

The best places to view the showers are away from the coast where clouds and fog are common during August, away from the bright lights of large cities and as high in elevation as you can get. If you are lucky enough to be backpacking in the High Sierra during the month you have the best view of all. Next to that, the best views are at the many park and forest service campgrounds in the Sierra and their foothills. From these you can have a clear view of the skies, little likelihood of clouds and the bright lights are far below you.

47

August
Shorttakes

BERRY PICKING TIME

Northern California doesn't have an abundance of wild berries, but the exotic Himalaya blackberry, the runners of which can grow up to sixty feet in a season, is found in large patches along the coast. These thick patches produce a prodigious amount of berries, and many people head for the backcountry roads where they can pick from the wild patches. Those who are lucky may also find patches of huckleberries that the birds and squirrels haven't already stripped in the redwood and fir forests.

VELVET TIME

Deer and elk are shedding the velvet of their new antlers during this month, and you can frequently see signs where they have rubbed their itchy antlers against a tree trunk. Sometimes you will actually see them in action.

MIGRATING SWALLOWS

By August large groups of swallows are congregating in preparation for their trip south. They band together in groups of a thousand or more as they get ready to head for their winter home in Mexico. Look for them where there are plenty of insects to feed on. The Sacramento/San Joaquin Delta is one area where they can generally be spotted.

UNUSUAL BIRDS

This is also the time you can watch for birds that are not normally seen in Northern California. Each year as birds begin their migrations south a few lose their way and end up far from where they should be. These are thought to have a form of dyslexia and take the wrong turn as they head south. Point Reyes National Seashore is a good place to look for these vagrants.

48

Breakout:
Migrating Pintails

Migrating waterfowl and the nippy days of autumn are so closely associated that few people realize the first flocks of migrating waterfowl reach the wildlife refuges of Northern California in the dog days of August. These are the pintail ducks, which begin their southern migration from the far reaches of North America in midsummer to reach their wintering grounds in South America.

They have completed their breeding season in the far north (although some nest in Northern California), and the summer's young swell the numbers of the flocks to spectacular proportions. Together the young and the old swoop down upon refuge ponds and surrounding farmlands to feed as they lay over on their long trip.

The national wildlife refuge system has long been geared toward providing breeding and feeding grounds for waterfowl—and all waterfowl aficionados should be thankful for that. Without the refuges we would have few waterfowl flying along the Pacific Flyway today. What were vast systems of wetlands in the Central Valley along the Sacramento and San Joaquin rivers and their tributaries, and the seasonal wetlands bordering the delta and the San Francisco Bay, have been drained and turned in to farmlands and cities.

Pescadero Marsh, the largest coastal marsh in central California, is a good place to see migrating birds.

Much of the wetlands that are left would have also have been lost but for the effort of a group generally despised by conservationists—hunters. Decades ago waterfowl hunters realized that the tremendous flocks of waterfowl that had traditionally migrated down three major flyways across the United States were slowly but surely decreasing. It was obvious that if the numbers continued to decrease at the same steady pace there would soon be no fowl to hunt.

At that point the hunters and conservationists realized they had a common goal—the protection of waterfowl habitat. Through their combined efforts such organizations as Ducks Unlimited, Isaac Walton League, Audubon Society, U.S. Fish and Wildlife Service and state fish and game commissions set aside large wetland sites along the flyways to provide the migrating waterfowl with feeding grounds.

It was only after large tracts of habitat were set aside that the groups realized there was also a need for protection of breeding grounds in the far north. This is an ongoing effort, and while the rate of decline in the waterfowl populations has slowed appreciably in the past decade or so, there is still much work to be done.

The northern pintail is one of the species that has benefited from these efforts, and their large populations continue to descend upon refuges and wetlands each August and stay for several months before continuing south.

HOTSPOTS

Not only is the pintail duck the earliest of the migrating waterfowl that stop over in California on their way south, it is also one of the least choosy in habitat. It is widespread throughout the northern part of the state on its layover, as just about any wet area is sufficient to attract this lovely fowl. Isolated lakes, marshland with shallow ponds, riparian sites with oxbow lakes and even baylands with salt and brackish water appeal to pintails. This makes it easy to find the pintail.

They are particularly plentiful at the three major national wildlife complexes in the state. In the far northeastern corner is the **Klamath Basin NWR Complex**, with the Upper Klamath, Tule Lake and Clear Lake NWRs. **Upper Klamath NWR** and **Tule Lake NWR** are especially good for viewing the pintails as you can use the canoe trails in these refuges to paddle into the midst of the large feeding groups for a close-up look at the pintails.

To reach the **Clear Lake** unit take CA 139 south from the town of Tulelake for 25 miles. Turn east on Clear Lake Road and continue 10 miles to the refuge.

For the Tule Lake unit go west on East-West Road out of Tulelake to its junction with Hill Road. Turn south on Hill for .5 mile to the visitors' center.

The visitors' center of the Lower Klamath unit is 4 miles north of Tulelake on CA 139 and 10 miles west on CA 161.

In the middle of the Sacramento Valley is the **Sacramento NWR** complex with the Sacramento, Delevan, Colusa and Sutter NWRs.

To reach the Sacramento unit take the Norman Road exit off I-5 about 5 miles south of Willows and return north along the frontage road for 2 miles to the refuge entrance.

Delevan NWR can be reached by taking the Maxwell exit off I-5. Take Maxwell Road 4 miles east to the refuge entrance.

Colusa NWR is .5 mile west of the town of Colusa on CA 20.

Sutter NWR is a bit more difficult to reach. From Yuba City take CA 99 south 5 miles to Oswald Road. Turn west on Oswald and go about 5 miles to Schlag Road. The parking lot is on the east levee of the Sutter Bypass, a controlled floodplain. The refuge lies in the bypass.

Of these refuges you can get closer to the ponds and birds in the Sacramento, but all offer excellent chances of seeing larger groups of feeding pintail.

Near the Sacramento NWR Complex are several state wildlife areas where viewing opportunities are as good, if not better, than in the national wildlife refuges. The best of these is **Gray Lodge Wildlife Area**, which is one of the most widely used and developed marshlands along the entire Pacific Flyway. **Butte Slough** and **Marysville Wildlife Areas** are less developed and do not have as large flocks of pintails as Gray Lodge, but also do not have as many people.

Gray Lodge is west of Gridley off CA 99. In Gridley take Colusa Road west to Pennington Road. Turn south and continue 1 mile to the refuge entrance.

For Butte Slough Wildlife Area take CA 20 west from Yuba City for 10 miles to West Butte Road. Turn north and go a little over 3.5 miles to the access road to the area.

Marysville Wildlife Area lies at the confluence of the Feather and Yuba rivers in Marysville and is the floodplain of Jack Slough and the Yuba River. You can reach it from a number of residential streets in northwest Marysville.

Farther south are the three units of the **Central San Joaquin Valley NWR Complex**. **San Luis NWR** has the largest concentration of waterfowl and **Kesterson NWR** is most famed for its high concentration of the natural trace

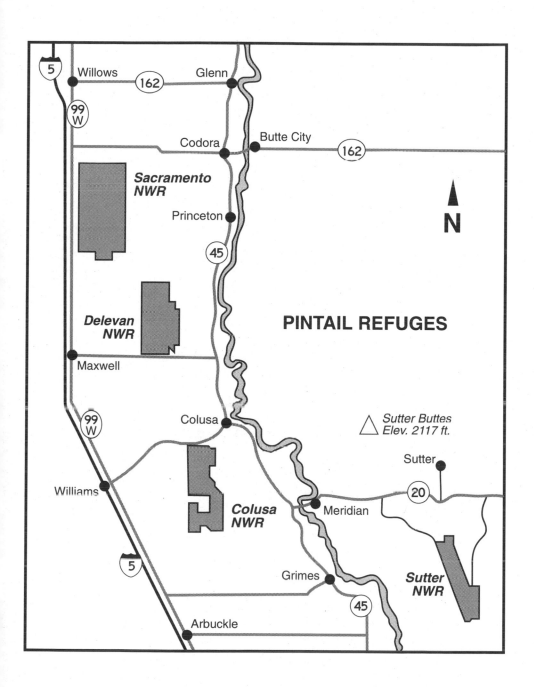

Willows
5
99 W
162
Glenn
Codora
Butte City
162
Sacramento NWR
Princeton
45
N
Delevan NWR
PINTAIL REFUGES
Maxwell
99 W
Colusa
△ Sutter Buttes
Elev. 2117 ft.
Sutter
Colusa NWR
20
Williams
Meridian
5
Grimes
45
Sutter NWR
Arbuckle

element selenium that leached from surrounding agricultural land into Kesterson's evaporation ponds. There the
natural trace element caused deformations in waterfowl
born in the refuge. **Merced NWR** is known for its flocks of
sandhill cranes and ring-necked pheasants.

All have large flocks of pintail ducks by late August,
and you can drive along levees to view these as they feed.

Kesterson is located 18 miles north of Los Banos and
4 miles east of Gustine on CA 140.

San Luis is located about 10 miles north of Los Banos.
Take CR J14 (also known as North Mercy Springs Road)
north for 8 miles to Wolfsen Road. Turn right and continue
2 miles to the refuge. This unit has higher concentrations of
pintails than either of the other two.

The Merced NWR is 8 miles south of Merced on CA 59
and the entrance to the refuge is a short distance west on
Sandymush Road.

Unlike many other waterfowl that migrate through
Northern California, the pintail is found in large numbers in
several other locations.

The 5-mile-wide **Eel River Delta** south of **Humboldt
Bay** is a one such stopover for pintail ducks, and it has the
added benefit of cool summer weather. While the temperatures at the wildlife refuge complexes in Modoc County and
the Sacramento/San Joaquin Valleys frequently rise above
100 degrees in August, that at the mouth of the Eel River
hovers between 65 and 75 degrees. Roads lead along both
sides of the delta, and the river itself winds through the delta.

To reach the north side of the delta take the Hookton
Road exit off U.S. 101 south of Eureka. You can reach the
Crab Park and Cock Robin Island area by taking the Loleta
exit to Loleta and then Cannibal Road west to Crab Park.

The south side of the delta is accessible from the
Fernbridge/Ferndale exit off U.S. 101. There are multiple
access points along the river.

SEPTEMBER

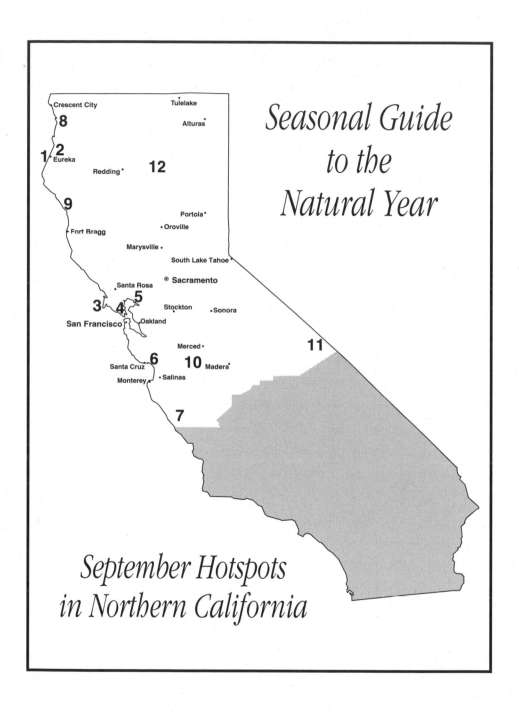

*Seasonal Guide
to the
Natural Year*

8

1 2
Eureka

Crescent City

Tulelake
Alturas

Redding 12

9

Portola
Oroville

Fort Bragg

Marysville

South Lake Tahoe

Santa Rosa

Sacramento

5

3 4

Stockton
Sonora

San Francisco
Oakland

Merced

11

6 10 Madera
Santa Cruz
Salinas
Monterey

7

*September Hotspots
in Northern California*

MAP SITE KEY

1. Humboldt Bay NWR
2. Arcata Marsh Wildlife Sanctuary
3. Point Reyes National Seashore
4. Rodeo Lagoon
5. Grizzly Island Wildlife Area
6. Moss Landing Wildlife Area
7. Lake San Antonio
8. Prairie Creek Redwoods SP
9. Sinkyone Wilderness SP
10. San Luis NWR
11. Owens Valley
12. Wild Horse Sanctuary

September Observations

49

Pelicans

The pelican is known as the bird "whose beak can hold more than its belly can," and there was genuine concern in the 1970s that regardless of how much food the brown pelican could capture in its beak it would go the way of the dodo. The pesticide DDT, which was the source for the decrease in the population of many raptors during the same period, so weakened the shells of pelican eggs that the large birds crushed them before they could hatch. The pelicans had gotten the insecticide from fish, their major food source.

Control of DDT has effectively remedied the reproduction problems of these large water birds, and they are no longer as threatened as they were in the 1970s and early 1980s. Today large flocks of pelicans can be seen at many areas along the coast of California, and breeding colonies are very active. The white pelican was never in as much danger as the brown and continues to thrive along the coast and at larger inland lakes.

The white pelican is by far the larger of the two species and can reach over 5 feet in length with a wing span of almost 10 feet. The smaller brown pelican reaches only a little over 4 feet in length with less than a 7-foot wing span. Both, however, are ponderous birds that fly in great flocks as they skim in line across the top of the water. Brown pelicans feed by plunging head first into the water to scoop up fish and crustaceans in their throat pouches. White pelicans are more sedate in their feeding habits as they swim on the surface of the water. They frequently work in groups as they scoop up fish and crustaceans by dipping their huge bills beneath the surface as they glide along.

Neither of the pelicans are noisy creatures, with adults only rarely emitting a low croak, but their nestlings do squeal as they ask for food.

Brown pelicans live only near salt water, where they often can be seen perching on posts and buoys. White pelicans live not only near salt water but also near inland lakes, where they can be seen slowly floating along the surface as they feed.

Both the brown and the white live year-round in Northern California, but the white seldom ventures north of San Francisco along the coast. The white has several nesting colonies inland at Klamath Basin and Mono Lake. During August you can see both at roosting sites around the state, where they are most active in the early morning and at dusk.

HOTSPOTS

Along the north coast in the **Arcata Marsh Wildlife Sanctuary** and the **Humboldt Bay NWR** the brown pelican is very active and seen in large numbers. The 154-acre sanctuary is one of the premier bird-watching spots along the coast, and dozens of species of birds can be seen there in a short visit.

Take Samoa Boulevard off U.S. 101 in Arcata and head west to "I" Street. Turn south on "I" and continue on it as it meanders through the marsh to the parking lot at its end. You should see brown pelicans all along the way. There are a number of pullouts for closer looks at large flocks.

The Humboldt Bay NWR includes over 20 miles of bayshore, and a wide diversity of bird species can be seen on any drive around the bay, among them the brown pelican.

From U.S. 101 in Eureka take CA 255 to Samoa and the north spit of the bay. To reach the south spit and Table Bluff Rock head south on U.S. 101 to Hookton Road. Head west on Hookton to Table Bluff Road, which turns into South Jetty Road. There are several vantage points of both the bay and the marsh along this road.

The northernmost spot along the coast where you can readily see white pelicans is on **Bird Rock** off **Tomales Point** in the **Point Reyes National Seashore**. Brown pelicans also roost in large numbers on the rock, which sits just offshore about 3 miles from the end of Pierce Ranch Road in the northern portion of the seashore.

From CA 1 just south of Point Reyes Station turn west on Sir Francis Drake Highway. Continue 2.5 miles to the Pierce Ranch Road intersection and turn north. The parking lot is 9 miles from the intersection. The Tomales Point Trail leads north from the parking lot.

A little more accessible spot is **Rodeo Lagoon** in the **Golden Gate National Recreation Area** just north of the Golden Gate Bridge in Marin County. An easy 2-mile trail leads around the lagoon and along the beach. Both white and brown pelicans are frequently seen here.

From U.S. 101 just north of the Golden Gate Bridge take the Conzelman Road exit to the Marin Headlands section of the Golden Gate National Recreation Area and go about 1 mile to McCullough Road. Take a right and continue for less than a mile to Bunker Road. Turn left on Bunker Road and continue to its end at the beach.

One of the largest concentrations of white pelicans in Northern California is found at the **Grizzly Island Wildlife Area** on Suisun Marsh each year in late summer and early fall. This area is a stopover point for millions of waterfowl and water birds each fall, but white pelicans have the most impressive flocks during September.

Take CA 12 east from I-80 near Suisun City and continue past the city to Grizzly Island Road. Make a right at Grizzly Island Road and continue for about 14 miles to the wildlife area. Check with the rangers for the best spots to view flocks of pelicans.

The largest roosting flocks of brown pelicans on the west coast congregate at the **Moss Landing Wildlife Area** each fall. Over seven thousand of these ponderous birds roost in the wildlife area, and they are most active in the early morning and at dusk each day.

The wildlife area adjoins **Moss Landing State Beach**, which lies on the north side of Elkhorn Slough as it enters Monterey Bay. The beach and wildlife area are about halfway between Santa Cruz and Monterey on the west side of CA 1.

Lake San Antonio in southern Monterey County is best known for its wintering flocks of bald eagles, but both brown and white pelicans flock to this prime feeding area in late summer and early fall.

From the north take the Jolon exit off U.S. 101 north of King City. Take CR G14 to the South Shore entrance to the park. Ask rangers for directions to the best sites for viewing pelicans.

50

Migrating Passerines

Many passerines, or perching birds, migrate to Central and South America for the winter. During the fall migration large flocks of these beautiful songbirds pass through Northern California on their way south. And fall is one of the best times to head outdoors along the coast, since the temperatures are moderate, the fog stays far offshore and the thick foliage of spring and summer begins to thin out as leaves turn and drop. This makes it easier to find warblers, flycatchers, gnatcatchers, thrushes, vireos and orioles, as well as many other species, as they feed on insects and fruit to build up their fat content for the long trip south.

The largest concentrations of migrating flocks are found along narrow peninsulas where the birds are funneled onto narrow strips of land. One such area is the Point Reyes Peninsula north of San Francisco. Geologically, Point Reyes is an island that has moved north from near Santa Barbara along the western edge of the San Andreas Fault over the past several million years to its present site off the Marin coast. Point Reyes is separated from the North American Plate along its southern end by Bolinas Lagoon, and along its northern end by Tomales Bay. The San Andreas Fault runs directly beneath these two waterways, which are separated by an isthmus of marsh and soil buildup that also connects Point Reyes to the mainland. As a result the island is temporarily a peninsula that extends out into the Pacific.

It also juts out into the migratory route of hundreds of species of songbirds. Its 100 square miles of varied and plentiful habitat are a welcome stopover spot for land birds that have been flying over the ocean. The varied habitats include many that are distinct and separate. With these variables you not only get large numbers of birds that are resting and feeding in distinct habitats, you also get predictable places to find them. Over 430 species of birds have been identified on Point Reyes. Many of these are vagrants, lost birds blown off course by storms or birds that suffer from a kind of migration dyslexia. Vagrants are particularly numerous during the fall when it is not unusual to see two or three birds a day generally seen only in the eastern portion of the United States.

Warblers are truly phenomenal here during the fall, when birders spot nineteen or twenty species in a single day—a count almost unheard of on the west coast.

HOTSPOTS

Within the **Point Reyes National Seashore** there are several very different sites where songbirds are present in large numbers. The first of these is near the visitors' center in **Bear Valley**. Forest and grassland birds are abundant near the picnic area, along Bear Creek and the Earthquake Trail and on some of the short trail loops that lead into the thick forests on the hillsides above Bear Valley.

There are several displays on birds in the visitors' center, and the rangers can give you information on the best places to see songbirds throughout the park.

The visitors' center is off Bear Valley Road, which closely parallels CA 1, about 6 miles north of Olema.

About halfway between Olema and the visitors' center is **Fivebrooks Trailhead**. From the trailhead parking lot meadowland and forest habitats are easily accessible.

The nearby pond, with plenty of riparian habitat, is another good birding site.

About a mile north of the visitors' center Limantour Road leads to the west. From the Sky Trail parking lot about a mile along Limantour you can take an easy walk into the woodlands of **Inverness Ridge** where various woodland species of songbirds are abundant. Farther along the road you come to the parking lot for **Limantour Beach**, where there are fewer songbirds, but plenty of shorebirds.

Bear Valley Road ends at Sir Francis Drake Highway. Take a left there to head into the interior of the park. The clumps of trees along the highway to **Drakes Beach** and the **Point Reyes Lighthouse** are the best spots to see vagrants. American redstarts, sage sparrows and MacGillivray's, black-and-white and Tennessee warblers have all been seen along this route.

Backtrack on Sir Francis Drake Highway to Pierce Ranch Road and take a left as you head north toward Tomales Point. A prime spot to see songbirds is at **Tomales Bay SP**, which lies between Pierce Ranch Road to the west and Tomales Bay to the east. A loop trail from Heart's Desire Beach takes you into woodlands where birders have been known to spot fifteen species in less than half an hour. Among the birds commonly seen there during fall migration are dark-eyed junco, lazuli bunting, purple finch and yellow warbler.

Along the southern edge of the park are the open grasslands of the marine terraces where warblers, finches, sparrows and flycatchers are abundant. The **Point Reyes Bird Observatory** has set up its **Palomarin Field Station** (see Chapter 45) here to study migrating patterns of land birds. From CA 1 at the north end of Bolinas Lagoon take the Olema-Bolinas Road a little over a mile to Mesa Road. Turn west on Mesa and continue for about 4 miles past the Coast Guard Station and the PRBO field station to the trailhead parking lot in the park. From there you can take several short hikes around the marine terrace to spot birds.

51

Rutting Elk

Bull elk begin calling together their harems of cow elk during late summer, and you can hear their high-pitched bugling from far distances. The bulls begin their call with a series of deep grunts that break into a high squeal that carries over vast expanses of grasslands. The bugles serve notice to any males who are infringing upon a bull's territory and challenges them to a fight if they do not heed the warning. It also calls wandering cows back to the harem.

Roosevelt elk bulls, the largest species of elk in California, can reach 1,000 pounds, while the smaller tule elk bulls are about half that at 500 pounds. Both are large beasts, however, that have been known to charge horses and cows that ignored their warning bugles. These charges don't have the suspense that battles between rutting bulls do. In these violent battles for dominance and territory competing bulls lower their heads and crash their majestic racks together. Elk racks can reach up to 5 feet in width, and bulls strain their powerful necks and legs as they manipulate their racks in an attempt to subdue their opponents.

Battles between bull elk seldom end in death—as the charges against ill-prepared horses and cows frequently do—but human observers do well to pay heed to the power and crankiness of bull elks during rutting season. Any observations should be done at a safe distance from bulls, and what constitutes safe often depends upon the irascibility of the nearby bulls. Stay a bit farther away than you think you need to be to protect yourself against a charging bull.

For at least ten thousand years the bugle of rutting elk rang over a range that extended almost coast to coast in America. Elk were by far the most widespread of the deer family in North America before the first Europeans arrived. This changed as a result of the western expansion in the United States as settlement and development destroyed the elk habitat. Elk were eliminated east of the Mississippi by the mid-1800s, and by 1900 less than 1 percent of the estimated ten million elk that lived in what is now the United States before the European invasion survived. Almost all of the approximately one hundred thousand elk in the United States at that time lived in the vast expanses of the Yellowstone ecosystem, both in and out of the park.

Although demands on the natural elk habitat continue, state and national parks, plus the U.S. Forest Service, provide protection for the expanding herds. Forest service lands alone provide a haven to over five hundred thousand elk on sixty-seven million acres of coniferous forests, timbered canyons and sagebrush flats. The most easily seen herds in California live in state and national parks, although several large herds also graze on forest service land.

HOTSPOTS

Elk herds have grown in leaps and bounds since the department of fish and game began reintroduction of the largest member of the deer family in California, and several large herds roam freely over public and private lands. Other herds are contained within the boundaries of large tracts of public lands. These are the places where you are most likely to get close enough to the rutting bulls to feel the power of these wild creatures.

Some of the most accessible herds of Roosevelt elk are found in **Prairie Creek Redwoods SP** along U.S. 101 between Arcata and Orick. Herds can be seen in the open prairie of the park along the highway and in the grass-covered dunes along much of Gold Bluffs Beach. The best times to hear bulls bugling are at dawn and dusk as the elk are more active feeding and moving around. Get out of your car, listen for the sounds of bugling and then move to get closer to the bulls with their harems.

Gold Bluffs Beach is reached from U.S. 101 by taking Davison Road west for about 7 miles.

Farther south is **Sinkyone Wilderness SP**, a hard-to-reach wilderness park where the herds are more dispersed. For those who want to see the large Roosevelt elk in a true wilderness setting, this is the place to go. A few narrow and steep roads offer access to this rugged park on the coast. A 17-mile-long trail stretches the length of the park, and you can reach the park from the south by CR 431, which heads west from CA 1 at milepost 90.88 between Leggett and the coast. From the north you take Briceland Road from Redway for 36 miles.

You can search for the herds as you hike along the park trails, but remember that bulls are very aggressive during rutting season. As you are hiking listen carefully for both bugles and the sounds of elk moving in the forests. When you hear either, try to ascertain how close you are and move accordingly.

At **Point Reyes National Seashore** are herds of the smaller tule elk. You can see young bulls as you reach the parking area at **Tomales Point Trailhead** at Pierce Ranch in the northern section of the seashore. For mature bulls who are collecting their harems and establishing their territories you need to hike along the trail that extends for about 4 miles

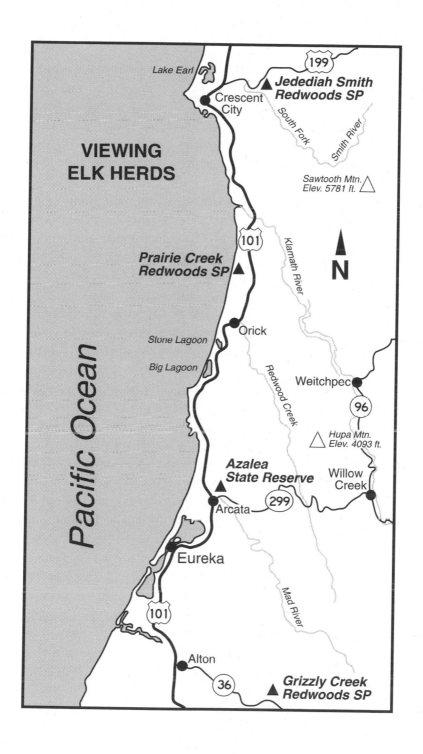

past Pierce Ranch. This is open country so you will be able to see the bulls and cows farther off than in some other parks, but there are also ridges and hollows where the herds are often hidden from sight until you reach a crest. Be careful that you do not inadvertently encounter a bull and startle him into attack.

The seashore lies along CA 1 to the north of Olema and south of Point Reyes Station. To reach the trailhead at Pierce Ranch, take Sir Francis Drake Highway from CA 1 and turn right on Pierce Ranch Road. The parking at the trailhead is 9 miles past the junction of Pierce Ranch Road and Sir Francis Drake Highway.

Grizzly Island Wildlife Area also has a herd of tule elk, and they graze on the back side of the duck ponds of the wildlife area. Plans are in the works for a wildlife viewing tower that will rise above the flat countryside. From there you will be able to see the elk herds as they migrate from pasture to pasture during the year. For now you will have to search for the herds from ground level and view them through binoculars or spotting scopes.

Grizzly Island Wildlife Area is on Suisun Bay, and you can reach it from I-80 near Suisun City by taking CA 12 east past Suisun City to Grizzly Island Road. Turn right on Grizzly Island and continue 14 miles to the game management headquarters. They will furnish you with current information about the herds.

San Luis NWR has another large herd of tule elk, and they can be viewed from the levees as you drive through the refuge.

The refuge is 10 miles north of Los Banos in the Central Valley. Take North Mercy Springs Road (CR J14) 8 miles to Wolfsen Road. Turn northeast and continue 2 miles to the refuge. You can drive along the top of the levees in search of elk.

Owens Valley is home to another of the big herds of tule elk in northern California, and you can get directions to it from the Department of Fish and Game. The herds are generally found in the sagebrush country that is part of the Bureau of Land Management lands to the south of Bishop, but they frequently move over large areas. A call to (619) 871-1171 will gain you further information about their current feeding grounds. Owens Valley is a large, wide valley that lies along U.S. 395 to the south of Bishop.

52

The Hunt
for Wild Horses

Wild horses, factually speaking, are not true wild animals. They are feral offspring of domesticated horses brought to the western United States by early conquistadors and explorers. These animals frequently escaped and adapted quickly to the wide-open range lands of the dry country that spread from the Rocky Mountains on the east to the Sierra Nevada on the west. There they filled an ecological niche that had been empty since the extinction of early horses that traveled in large herds across the plains of North America long ago in prehistoric times.

Over the years these herds grew and eventually began to compete with both native wildlife and ranchers for the scarce forage that grew in this region of low rainfall. Unfortunately for the wild mustang, most of the land where they roam is under the jurisdiction of the U.S. Bureau of Land Management. For decades this agency has managed most of the open range under its control for large cattle ranchers, who get inexpensive grazing permits allowing their herds to roam over vast acreages.

Even with large amounts of land there is precious little forage for the number of grazing cattle, and something had to give. The cattle had their own built-in lobby, and the large animals native to the range had conservationists fighting for protection of their habitat. The mustangs had no one. At least, no one very powerful.

In the 1960s a mustang eradication program was initiated by the bureau in which large herds of mustangs were rounded up and killed. This brought out animal rights advocates who insisted there had to be a better way of controlling the wild horse population on the western ranges. As a result, the Bureau of Land Management began the "Adopt-A-Horse" program in the 1970s. This program was designed to find homes for mustangs rounded up from bureau land.

One couple, Jim and Diane Clapp, became involved with these roundups, believing the mustangs would be adopted through the new program. What they found was that at least sixty horses in the herd they collected were slated for the slaughterhouse. The Clapps were violently opposed to the slaughter of the animals, and that spurred them into action. They declared they would find a sanctuary where the horses could roam free as they had for generations. From that came the Wild Horse Sanctuary near Shingletown, outside Red Bluff.

Since 1983, the Clapps have overseen the 5,000-acre preserve where over two hundred wild mustangs have been given a refuge. In recent years the Clapps have added some of a rare breed of Spanish Barb horses called the Cruce Herd. These wild horses are from Spanish colonial days and were thought to be extinct until recently. They are the oldest documented strain from which the wild horses that roam the American west descended.

The sanctuary is one of only three in the United States, and it gives visitors an opportunity to see a remnant of the old west. Two- and three-day horse pack trips are offered into the pristine backcountry of the preserve where riders in search of the elusive herds can follow trails wild horses have cut through the scrub oak and chaparral. The best time to take one of these trips is in September after the worst of the summer heat has passed and the evenings are cool.

Black Butte, Mt. Lassen and Mt. Shasta all stand high above the horizon and are visible as you ride along the trails to the rustic camps where you spend evenings around a campfire listening to tales of the sanctuary and wild horses. You may even hear mustangs slurping water from a nearby vernal pool as you prepare for bed.

The Bureau of Land Management policy of controlling or eradicating wild horse populations and the conservationists idea of controlling feral animals are both lacking, as far as I am concerned. It's true that the mustangs of the west are the descendants of domesticated horses, yet they have thrived for almost five hundred years in a habitat that had supported wild horses in previous times. How long do they have to survive in this hostile environment to qualify as an indigenous animal? Maybe it is time that we treat the wild horses and burros of the arid regions of the west as we do other large animals such as the desert bighorn sheep. Let them live and compete for their niche in the habitat with other native animals, and may the fittest survive. That is much what the Clapps are doing at the Wild Horse Sanctuary, and it seems to be working.

The Wild Horse Sanctuary is located between Red Bluff and Lassen Volcanic NP off I-5. Take the second Red Bluff exit heading north off I-5 toward Lassen. Turn left at the second Lassen sign on CA 36 and continue 10 miles to Dale's Station. Turn left there to Manton and then take another left at Manton Corner's Store. Follow the road toward Shingletown for another 3.5 miles to the Wild Horse Sanctuary.

53

September Shorttakes

POISON OAK

September is a good time to look out for poison oak, not to avoid it, but to enjoy its bright red leaves as they change from shiny green before they fall. Poison oak takes many forms in this region, from low brush to long vines. In the Sierra foothills it most often grows in large thickets of stalks that reach up to 10 feet in height, and these turn whole hillsides red when their leaves change in the fall. Near the coast the red leaves can often be seen one hundred or more feet up a redwood or fir tree where the red leaves stand in stark contrast to the green needles of the trees.

FLOCKS OF STARLINGS

During harvest time flocks of thousands of starlings head for the fields to pick over the ripe crops. In wine country they are considered to be real pests that consume tons of premium grapes, and in the Central Valley they feed on the leftovers of the harvest. These black imports from Great Britain may be pests, but they are one of the few songbirds that we still can see in such large flocks.

VINEYARDS

This is also the time to head for vineyard country in both the Central Valley and in Napa and Sonoma counties to view the grape vines as their leaves turn and create the most colorful fields in California. For those who bemoan the lack of fall color in California, the vineyards are a treat.

54

Breakout: Point Reyes Bird Observatory

Migrating birds are indicator species that provide scientists with valuable information about the condition of the environment. More than 250 species of North American birds winter in Central and South American tropical forests, and researchers at the Point Reyes Bird Observatory north of San Francisco are providing much needed information about species that migrate along the Pacific Flyway to Central and South America each fall through their netting and banding program.

One of a handful bird observatories, and the oldest in North America, PRBO is run by scientists who utilize a corps of volunteers. The volunteers string nearly invisible mist nets across the landscape like curtains to catch small migrating birds without harming them. After birds are removed from the nets they are placed in cloth sacks and taken back to the base station. There vital information such as age and general condition of the birds is recorded, and a small, numbered identification band is placed onto a leg of each bird. If that bird is ever recaptured, either at PRBO or another site, valuable information about migratory patterns can be compiled.

Bird banding such as that done at PRBO is not new or unusual. Since the 1920s more than forty million birds of a wide variety of species have been banded. The information gathered from recovered banded birds has been combined with long-term information gained from the Audubon Christmas Bird Count and the U.S. Fish and Wildlife Service Breeding Bird Survey. This provides scientists with statistics about bird ecosystems that are being correlated with nonbird information to give us a better understanding of the interaction between ecosystems thousands of miles apart.

In recent decades biologists and ornithologists have charted steady and sometimes drastic declines in the recovery of banded birds. This has led to further research into the relationship of bird populations and the health of various ecosystems. For example, a Swainson's thrush, which breeds in California, depends upon a wide range of complex ecosystems each year to survive. In late summer and early fall, after they have raised the year's brood, the thrush joins others in large flocks that head south. They feed on insects and fruit along streamside habitats as they begin their arduous journey to their winter feeding grounds. Without a good supply of insects and fruit the thrushes will not be able to store the fat they need for their migration south.

By late September the thrushes will join with even larger mixed flocks of songbirds as they all follow the Pacific Flyway to Central America. Many of the thousands of miles flown by the birds will be at night, and when the thrushes arrive at their winter feeding grounds they will be exhausted and in need of nourishment. If the forest where they wintered the previous year has been slashed and burned they may not be strong enough to find another feeding ground before they die of starvation.

With luck the thrushes will make it through the winter, and will return north in the spring to their California breeding grounds. Many songbirds—and the Swainson's thrush appears to be one of them—are site specific. This means they rely upon a specific place or habitat for breeding year after year. For example, one banded warbling vireo returned to the same streamside breeding site at Point Reyes for thirteen straight seasons.

If the habitat where the thrushes return to nest has been destroyed or disturbed, whether by agricultural expansion or urban development, the thrush will not breed. This will cause even further decline in the songbird population.

PRBO, along with other bird observatories throughout the nation, is collecting data to help us diagnose the general health of our environment through their study of songbird migration. Sometimes even the scientists at the observatories are surprised by their discoveries. In the spring of 1986 researchers at PRBO were looking over banding data. They discovered a dramatic drop (up to 60 percent) in the number of birds hatching from nests of breeding pairs of some species. On further examination the researchers connected the decline with May rains that had fallen from clouds contaminated with radioactivity from the Chernobyl nuclear power plant disaster earlier in the year. Researchers tested dead birds found in the area and found that tissue from the birds was "hot" from radiation.

That is just the type of necessary information that ornithologists know bird banding research can provide to help the general public understand the state of the health of the environment. And *you* can participate in this research. PRBO uses a number of volunteers year-round, and it is always on the lookout for sincere and dedicated people who can work with captured birds.

The headquarters of PRBO are at Stinson Beach, but the Palomarin Field Station, where all the banding work is done, is located at the southern end of the Point Reyes National Seashore. Visitors are welcome at the field station, even if you do not want to volunteer, and you can observe the workers as they remove the birds from the mist nets and band them.

To reach the field station take the Olema-Bolinas Road off CA 1 at the northern end of Bolinas Lagoon. Don't expect to find signs to Bolinas. The highway department periodically places signs at this intersection but they seldom last more than a few days before they are removed. The residents of this small coastal community seem to like their privacy and don't encourage outsiders to visit.

Go 1 mile on Olema-Bolinas Road to Mesa Road. Turn right on Mesa and continue for about 4 miles past the Coast Guard Station and into the Point Reyes National Seashore. Park near the field station.

OCTOBER

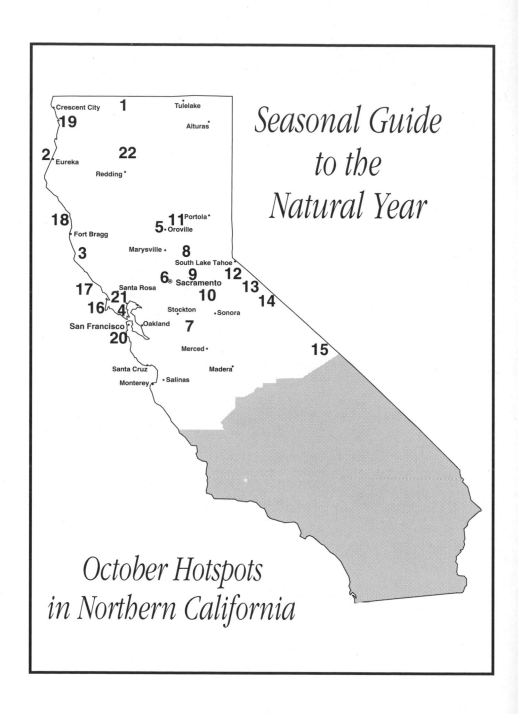

Crescent City 19 1 Tulelake
Alturas
2 Eureka 22
Redding
18 11 Portola
Fort Bragg 5 Oroville
3 Marysville 8
South Lake Tahoe
17 6 9 12
Santa Rosa Sacramento 13
21 10 14
16 4 Stockton Sonora
San Francisco Oakland 7
20
Merced
Santa Cruz Madera
Monterey Salinas
15

Seasonal Guide to the Natural Year

October Hotspots in Northern California

MAP SITE KEY

1. Bogus Creek
2. Mad River Hatchery
3. Van Damme SP
4. Samuel P. Taylor SP
5. Feather River Hatchery
6. Nimbus Fish Hatchery
7. Tuolumne River
8. Nevada City/Grass Valley
9. Coloma/Placerville
10. Sonora/Jamestown
11. Feather River Highway—CA 70
12. Carson and Luther Pass Region
13. Monitor Pass
14. Walker River Canyon
15. Bishop Area
16. Point Reyes National Seashore
17. Sonoma Coast State Beaches
18. Mendocino Beaches
19. Humboldt Lagoons SP
20. Pescadero State Beach
21. Hawk Hill
22. Lake Shasta

October Observations

55

Salmon Runs

The Native Americans who lived near the major waterways of Northern California looked forward to fall, for that was the time they could concentrate on catching one of their staple foods—salmon. Each fall king, coho and steelhead salmon left the open ocean where they had spent several years maturing and entered the fast-flowing rivers of Northern California. They were headed far upstream to spawn, and the natives knew they could depend upon taking great catches of these large and bountiful fish as they entered shallow waters near rapids and falls. As the salmon fought the river flow on their migration upstream they became vulnerable to the hooks, nets and spears of the natives who waited along the riverbanks.

Today the large native tribes are gone, as are the tremendous migrations of salmon. Both were victims of modern civilization, but in the long run the salmon may fare better than the natives. The many tribes who lived and prospered in the fertile lands of what is now California have been pushed to extermination, or near to it. Those left have retained only a few of their traditional practices, and no longer do whole villages congregate along the shores of the Eel, the Mad, the Klamath, the Sacramento and the American rivers to catch their winter's rations.

In their place large numbers of urban and suburban dwellers congregate at fish ladders and hatcheries along the same rivers to watch the small numbers of salmon that make their way upstream to dams and other modern contrivances, where they are diverted into unnatural environments to be milked of their eggs. These eggs will be carefully hatched in controlled environments and later released into the rivers. From there the salmon will make their migrations to the ocean where they will stay, feed and grow to maturity. They will then return to the rivers in search of spawning grounds.

Unfortunately, the number of returning salmon along northern California rivers is steadily decreasing. Whether this is from poor survival of hatchery-raised salmon or factors beyond the control of the fish and wildlife personnel is not clearly understood. The fact remains that the annual spawning runs of salmon along northern California rivers are getting smaller year after year, and if you wish to get a glimpse of this natural spectacle before it completely disappears, do it soon.

In their natural state salmon struggled to the upper reaches of rivers where they laid their eggs on the gravel bottoms before they died. In their unnatural state they struggle to the mid-reaches of these same rivers where they enter fish ladders that take them into hatcheries where humans strip their eggs from them and hatch them under controlled conditions. And that is what you are most likely to see as you search for spawning salmon.

You can still get a glimpse of what Native American fishermen took for granted, though, if you head downstream from the fish ladders. There you can see the salmon fighting their way upstream to spawning grounds that were imprinted upon the salmons' brains in times long forgotten. This battle to reach shallow water with gravel bottoms where fertilized eggs can hatch has gone on for so many generations that it is unforgivable that humans have built barriers prohibiting the salmon from ever reaching true spawning grounds.

Steel tanks and humans who strip unfertilized roe from female salmon and sperm from males simply are not an acceptable substitute. Here's hoping there are still salmon around to make that push upstream to spawning grounds long after the dams that now form unbeatable barriers have disappeared.

HOTSPOTS

The California Department of Fish and Game operates the largest hatchery system in the United States, and while hatcheries cannot match the attraction of wild, undammed rivers as spawning grounds, they are marvels in their own right. The ladders and hatcheries that sit alongside once-wild rivers produce over fifty million fish for stocking streams and rivers throughout the state each year. These include over twenty-five million salmon that are released in rivers where they can head for the open waters of the Pacific Ocean.

It is the yearly return of these salmon to their spawning grounds that is the spectacle attracting both fishermen and nonfishermen to the banks of Northern California rivers in large numbers each fall. For the nonfishermen most excitement is found near the hatcheries around the state.

The **Klamath River** is still one of the premier salmon spawning rivers in California, but it is far from the reproductive system it was before the first dam was built on its upper reaches in 1910. Before the Copco Dam No. 1 was completed at mile 198 in 1910, salmon migrated over 270 miles upstream above Klamath Falls, Oregon to spawn. After it was completed the last 70 or so miles of spawning streams were cut off from the salmon. In 1960 Iron Gate Dam was completed at mile 190 to cut off another 8 miles of tributaries the salmon could reach.

That left **Bogus Creek** as the uppermost tributary along the Klamath where the salmon could spawn naturally. Today five thousand to six thousand adult salmon enter

Bogus Creek to spawn each fall, and pairs can be seen everywhere along the first 5 miles of the small (10–12 feet wide and only a couple of feet deep) creek during spawning season.

Just upstream from the confluence of Bogus Creek and the Klamath River sits Iron Gate Dam. Built by the Pacific Power and Light Company in the late 1950s, the dam further restricted the upstream movement of migrating salmon, and in 1966 the **Iron Gate Salmon and Steelhead Hatchery** was opened.

After a walk along Bogus Creek to see spawning salmon in their natural state you can drive to the hatchery to see the modern facility.

Take the Hornbrook exit off I-5 about 15 miles north of Yreka and follow the Klamath River upstream 8 miles to Iron Gate Dam. You can park at the hatchery and walk back downriver to Bogus Creek to see natural spawning before returning to the hatchery to watch its modern equivalent.

The **Mad River Hatchery** sits along the Mad River near Blue Lake not far inland from Humboldt Bay. To reach the hatchery take CA 299 east from Arcata to the Blue Lake turnoff. Turn right on Greenwood Avenue, left on Railroad Avenue, and then right on Hatchery Road in town. Take Hatchery Road across the Mad River and continue 1.5 miles to the hatchery.

For spawning sites that are not connected with a hatchery there are several coho, or silver, salmon runs along the coast. You can walk along the **Little River** in **Van Damme SP** or along **Lagunitas Creek** in **Samuel P. Taylor SP** in Marin County to watch the salmon battle their way upstream. Van Damme SP is located off CA 1 about 2 miles south of the village of Mendocino and Samuel P. Taylor SP is located along Sir Francis Drake Boulevard between Larkspur along U.S. 101 and Olema along CA 1.

The **Feather River Hatchery** was constructed after Oroville Dam was built in the late 1950s for flood control

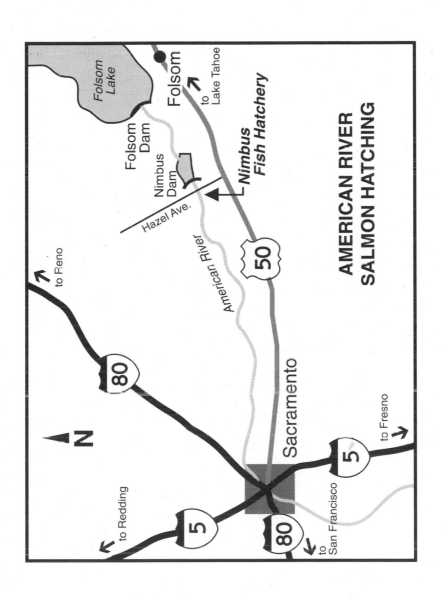

AMERICAN RIVER
SALMON HATCHING

along the Feather River. The hatchery includes an observation platform and underwater window where you can view the spawning operation. The hatchery sits near downtown Oroville along the Feather River.

Near Sacramento you can see salmon heading upstream to spawn on the American River. The **American River Parkway** offers many access points along the river where you can see the large salmon passing by, and the **Nimbus Fish Hatchery** offers tours of their facility. You can observe salmon climbing fish ladders to the hatchery and hatchery activities. Take the Hazel Avenue exit off U.S. 50 about 20 miles east of downtown Sacramento and follow the signs to the hatchery.

Another spot where you can view natural spawning activities is along the **Tuolumne River** between Waterford and La Grange in the San Joaquin Valley. There are several public access points along CA 132 (called Yosemite Boulevard, between the two small communities) east of Modesto off CA 99.

56

Fall Color Tours

In the introduction I talked about the myths of California and its lack of seasons. Well, another myth is that there is no fall color in California. It's true that the vast hardwood forests that turn hues of deep reds, yellows and oranges in the fall don't exist in the state, but that doesn't mean there is no color. You just have to look a little farther afield than Main Street.

The temperate Coastal and Central Valley regions of Northern California frequently do not have the sharp cold snaps required to quickly drain the chlorophyll from the foliage, causing them to reveal their true colors before they fall to the ground. You gain elevation as you ascend to the Sierra Nevada foothills, though, and there you begin to get the warm days and cool nights that bring about fall color. Many leaves continue to produce sugar during the warm sunny days of early fall, but the cool to cold nights prevent the movement of the sugar from the leaves. Red and yellow pigments then build up in the leaves to create the brilliant colors of autumn.

Maples, deciduous oaks, redbud and flowering dogwood produce the various hues of red and yellow that line river canyons throughout the gold rush country, and these offer some the best places to see fall colors in northern California.

From the foothills you can head for the high passes of the Sierra, where more color is present since frosts arrive suddenly and early at the higher elevations. There are not as many reds in the forests there, but the vibrant gold leaves of the large groves of quaking aspen more than make up for the lack of diversity.

HOTSPOTS

In general, you find better fall colors as you reach higher elevations. The first region that offers good color, and one that is popular for fall drives, is along CA 49 in the gold rush country. There you will see the light reds and oranges of various oaks, redbud and dogwood, plus the yellow of maples as they add splashes of color on the slopes of river canyons. Exotics add more color as you drive through the historic towns that extend from Mariposa in the south to Sierraville in the north. Along much of this route oak woodlands, chaparral and open grasslands dominate the countryside and fall colors are somewhat a hit-and-miss affair. As you follow highways through the many river canyons you will most assuredly discover a treasure of color as transitory as the gold that first brought Europeans to the region. The colors begin earlier on the northern end of CA 49, and last later as you continue south to Mariposa.

You can center your color tours around such historic areas as **Nevada City/Grass Valley** to the north, **Coloma/Placerville** and **Sonora/Jamestown** in the middle and **Mariposa** to the south. From these delightful towns, many of them with restored historic downtowns, you can take day drives on winding mountain roads where steep slopes rise above rivers and streams. The best views are across the rivers from the roads.

Farther north is Feather River country, where CA 70 follows the picturesque **Feather River Canyon** as it snakes through the mountains from Oroville to Quincy. Along the river there are plenty of maple, oak and small shrubs that turn various hues during the fall, making this one of the most pleasant drives in the state. The timing of fall colors varies along this route, so call the Plumas National Forest head-quarters at (916) 283-2050 to find out when and where the colors are best.

Or you can head up to the passes high in the **Sierra Nevada**, and reach elevations where the gold leaves of the quaking aspen are more predictable. These striking trees, which offer spots of green as they bud in the spring and are the lone deciduous groves among the vast evergreen forests of the high country, turn a "can't miss" gold as the first frosts strike in the fall. Then a drive through the high passes provides panoramic vistas dominated by the large groves of golden aspen. In some areas these are visible for miles, while in others small groves are a wonderful surprise as you turn a bend in the highway and come upon them suddenly and unexpectedly.

Two of the best drives in the mid-Sierra are along CA 89 from U.S. 50 near Lake Tahoe to the junction with CA 88 in the middle of Hope Valley and along CA 88 from Woodfords to Silver Lake over Carson Pass.

Just a little farther south you can follow CA 89 from Woodfords through Markleeville and over Monitor Pass to U.S. 395. This route passes by some of the largest groves of aspen in the region. Several of these blanket distant slopes that bring cars to grinding halts as the panoramas come into view.

U.S. 395 follows the **Walker River Canyon** south from Walker to Devils Gate Summit and then continues south through Bridgeport and over Conway Summit. This whole route is lined with scattered groves of colorful aspen, cottonwood, dogwood and willow, and CA 108, which heads west to Sonora Pass about halfway between Walker and Bridgeport and passes through large groves of aspen on its way to the 9,624-foot pass.

Just north of **Conway Pass** is a large grove of colorful aspen just to the west of U.S. 395 that is visible from a scenic roadside stop, and the **Virginia Lakes Road**, which heads west into a subalpine region just before Conway Summit, heads into an area noted for its fall colors. The road dead-ends at a chain of lakes at 9,500 feet in elevation, and fall generally comes early in the month here.

The drive up CA 120 from Lee Vining to Tuolumne Meadows over **Tioga Pass** leads through large groves of willow and cottonwood.

Farther south and a little later in the month, the colors are as brilliant as anywhere in the west. The Bishop Chamber of Commerce sponsors the annual **Bishop Fall Color Festival** and provides a free map to the best color sites in the area. Call the chamber at (619) 873-8405 for information about the festival and the fall colors. The U.S. Forest Service has a toll-free fall color hotline where you can get up-to-the-minute information on the best places in the national forests to see colors. The number is (800) 354-4595.

57

Late Summer Beaches

It may seem odd to be talking about late summer beaches in October, when much of the rest of the country is enjoying cool fall weather. Some regions have even had several hard frosts by mid-October. The truth is, however, that often the warmest and most pleasant month to visit Northern California beaches is October. And the fact that the traditional summer crowds have long since vanished to leave the beaches virtually free of visitors makes this a great time to take solitary walks along long stretches of sand.

The beaches are also different in early fall. The gentle waves of summer have left wide deposits of sand near the shore, and the beaches are broader and flatter than they will be after the heavy waves of winter storms return. These powerful waves with their pounding breakers will carry the sand back offshore where it will become sandbars on the offshore shelves, waiting to be returned to the beaches during the following summer.

This cyclical process leaves the broadest beaches at the end of the summer season, and it is then that you will find the best beach walking of the year. The fog that shrouds the north coast during the summer lies far offshore during the quiet days of fall, and the winds that forewarn the coming

The white cliffs above Drakes Beach are reminiscent of those at Dover, England.

of winter storms are yet to come. No wind, no fog, warm sunny days and wide, uncrowded beaches add up to pleasant outings from Big Sur to the Oregon border.

California gulls returning with their summer fledglings and migrating water and shore birds collecting in lagoons and along the quiet beaches provide great birdwatching to go with the pleasant hikes.

HOTSPOTS

Anyone who likes the ocean and has lived in California for very long knows that this is the premier time to head for the beaches, so your best chances of avoiding others is to go to beaches away from the cities. But you don't have to head very far. While Ocean or Baker beaches in San Francisco may be heavily used during October, excellent beaches both to the north and south of the city will be empty of people.

Drakes, Limantour, Point Reyes, Kehoe and **McClure's beaches** in **Point Reyes National Seashore** are nearly empty during this month. Two-mile-long Limantour

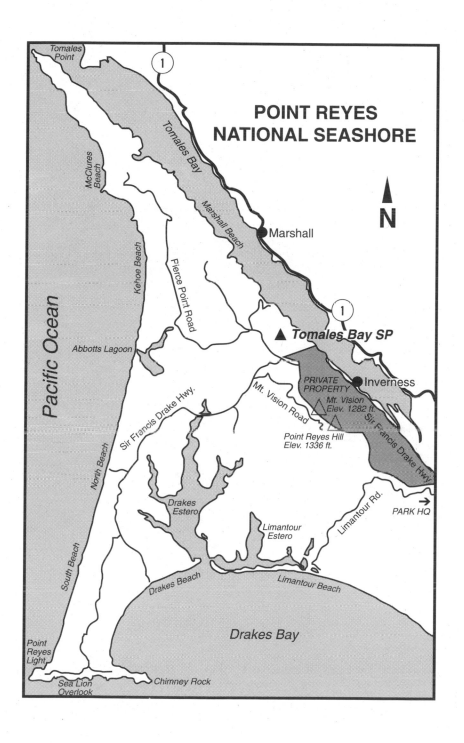

POINT REYES
NATIONAL SEASHORE

N

Tomales
Point

McClures
Beach

Tomales Bay

Marshall Beach

Kehoe Beach

Pierce Point Road

Pacific Ocean

• Marshall

Abbotts Lagoon

Sir Francis Drake Hwy.

Mt. Vision Road

▲ Tomales Bay SP

PRIVATE
PROPERTY

Mt. Vision
Elev. 1282 ft.

• Inverness

Sir Francis Drake Hwy.

North Beach

Point Reyes Hill
Elev. 1336 ft.

Drakes
Estero

Limantour
Estero

Limantour Rd.

→
PARK HQ

South Beach

Drakes Beach

Limantour Beach

Point
Reyes
Light

Drakes Bay

Sea Lion
Overlook

Chimney Rock

Beach, one of the longest stretches of sand along the west coast, lies at the end of Limantour Road about 10 miles off Bear Valley Road between Olema and Sir Francis Drake Highway.

Drakes Beach lies just across the mouth of Drakes Estero from the end of Limantour spit, but you reach it by Sir Francis Drake Highway from CA 1 just south of Point Reyes Station. Follow the signs to Drakes Beach, which is 14 miles from CA 1. The white cliffs that rise above the wide beach here are reminiscent of the cliffs of Dover, which is appropriate since this is where Sir Francis Drake supposedly laid over with his crew from the *Golden Hind* during the sixteenth century.

There are two roads that lead to **Point Reyes Beach**, both off Sir Francis Drake Highway. The road to North Beach leads west about 2 miles before you reach the turnoff to Drakes Beach. The road to South Beach is about 2 miles past the turnoff. Although the signs designate North Beach and South Beach, Point Reyes Beach is really one long beach that extends over 10 miles from Point Reyes Lighthouse on the south to McClure's Beach on the north.

Abbott's Lagoon and **Kehoe Beach** are two other access points to this long strand. Both trailheads are off Pierce Ranch Road, which heads north off Sir Francis Drake Highway about 2.5 miles from CA 1. The trail to Abbott's lagoon is about 2 miles long, and the one to Kehoe Beach is less than a mile.

The final access to this long beach is at **McClure's Beach**. The parking to the beach is at the end of Pierce Ranch Road, and a half-mile-long trail leads to the beach from the parking area.

Farther north the **Sonoma Coast State Beaches** extend from Bodega Bay on the south to Goat Rock on the north. Along this 13-mile stretch of CA 1 there are a number of beaches, but the longest is 3-mile-long **Salmon Creek Beach**. Plenty of waterbirds use the lagoon at the mouth of

Salmon Creek as a layover during migration. The beach at **Goat Rock** also offers a good walk, plus you can watch the harbor seals that haul out at the mouth of the Russian River, which may be closed off by a sand spit to form a large lagoon.

In Mendocino County, **Manchester Beach SP** lies to the west of CA 1 about a mile north of Point Arena. **McKerricher SP** also lies to the west of CA 1 but about 2 miles north of Fort Bragg. Both have long stretches of beach for solitary walks.

The best beach to hike along the far north coast is at **Big Lagoon** in the **Humboldt Lagoons SP**. About 15 miles north of Trinidad, follow the signs to Big Lagoon. You can hike for miles along the wild beach or explore around the lagoon where many migrating waterbirds lay over.

Heading south of San Francisco the best beaches for hikes are **Pescadero State Beach**, about 20 miles south of Half Moon Bay along CA 1; **Año Nuevo State Reserve**, along CA 1 about 15 miles north of Santa Cruz and **Carmel River State Beach** just south of Carmel. These are more likely to have other hikers on them than beaches farther north but are still far from crowded.

58

Hawk Hill and Migrating Raptors

Each fall there is an invasion of the Marin Headlands across the Golden Gate from San Francisco. The headlands jut out into the Pacific Ocean here, and just about every raptor that migrates south along the coast is funneled across the narrow bit of the Marin Peninsula where the Pacific Ocean and San Francisco Bay join at the Golden Gate.

Bald eagles, ospreys and peregrine falcons—along with red-tailed, red-shouldered, rough-legged and marsh hawks—are among the nineteen species of raptors that are regularly seen at Hawk Hill off Conzelman Road during the migrating season. In 1976 a twentieth species, the Mississippi Kite, was spotted heading south.

The sightings at Hawk Hill each year rival those at the more famous Hawk Mountain in Pennsylvania, and as at Hawk Mountain a group of volunteers have joined together to record them. The Golden Gate Raptor Observatory has about 150 volunteers who assist a paid director in making, recording and interpreting observations. Several volunteers also lead outings to help novices observe the migrating raptors.

After the raptors pass over the Golden Gate they continue down the San Francisco Peninsula, and a prime viewing spot to the south of the city is Sweeny Ridge, also a part of the Golden Gate National Recreation Area. In addition to being an ideal spot for viewing migrating raptors, Sweeny Ridge is of historical interest. It was from its vantage point that the Gaspar de Portola expedition became the first Europeans to see San Francisco Bay in 1769.

To reach Hawk Hill take the first exit north of the Golden Gate Bridge off U.S. 101 and take the first left to wind back beneath the freeway to Conzelman Road and the Marin Headlands section of the Golden Gate National Recreation Area. Follow Conzelman a winding 4 miles to the top of the ridge. Park at any of several pull-outs and watch the raptors soar around the hills, many at eye level. There are also several well-marked trails that lead you away from the crowds beside the road.

For Sweeny Ridge take Skyline Boulevard south out of San Francisco to Skyline College. Turn west onto the college campus, then left at the first intersection. Parking Lot No. 2 is the first parking lot on the left. This is open to visitor parking, and the trail to Sweeny Ridge leads from the rear of the lot. It is a strenuous 2-mile hike to the San Francisco Bay Discovery Site, but you reach prime raptor viewing within less than a mile.

59

October
Shorttakes

SQUIRREL ACTIVITY

This is the time when you can hear gray squirrels *chunk-chunking* as they establish their territory in the tall pine trees of the Sierra. You can easily find signs of squirrel activity as you walk along the open understory of the ponderosa and sugar pine forests. Cores of eaten cones abound on the forest floor, and you are likely to hear cones falling around you as the small chicory squirrels toss them to the ground where they can chew without having to hold the large cones.

HIKING IN THE FALL

Few people think of fall as the time for day hikes in the Sierra, for the weather has a nip to it, and there is no reason to escape the heat of the Central Valley, but I find it one of the most enjoyable times to head to the Sierra. The trails are almost empty, the weather is nippy but not cold, and the seasonal changes are apparent in the flora.

PELAGIC BIRDING TRIPS

This is one of the best times to take boat trips out of Monterey to view the large flocks of pelagic birds that congregate at the rich feeding grounds of the outer Monterey Bay. Several tour groups are located in Monterey and lead regularly scheduled trips.

PUMPKIN FIELDS

For a bit of color, head for the coastal counties and their large pumpkin fields. Many of these have traditional farm activities such as blacksmithing and sewing and cooking demonstrations to go along with pumpkin sales.

60

Breakout: Houseboating in the Off-Season

Four rivers—the Pit, Squaw, McCloud and Sacramento—join to form the four arms of Shasta Lake in Northern California. Including the large lake that lies immediately behind Shasta Dam and the four arms that reach far up the rivers feeding Shasta Lake, there are over 350 miles of shoreline that can be best explored by boat.

Shasta is one of two premier houseboating regions in Northern California—the other is the Sacramento/San Joaquin Delta—and during the hot summers of the Sacramento Valley the lake is filled with enough houseboats, waterskiing boats and fishing boats to form huge traffic jams at narrow channels. The smallest coves are seldom free of houseboats overnight, and the open expanses of mid-lake are so filled with racing ski boats during midday that you place yourself in serious jeopardy by venturing into the traffic.

All these combine to make Shasta a less than satisfactory destination to explore nature in solitude during the peak boating months. As the weather begins to cool and families return home to enroll their children in school, the boating population of this large lake drops dramatically. Houseboating then becomes a perfect way to explore the many coves and inlets of all four arms of the lake. There you can see deer browsing near the water's edge, hear wild burros braying on the hillsides above and see egrets and herons feeding along the shore.

On the McCloud River arm of the lake you can spend your nights in coves surrounded by craggy cliffs, while by day you can explore caves such as Samwell Cave, which is accessible via a mile-long trail from Point McCloud.

The Squaw Creek arm leads to some of the most beautiful areas on the lake with rolling hills where driftwood collects on the gentle slope of the shoreline, and you can take leisurely hikes on the oak-studded hillsides. Near the mouth of the Squaw Creek arm between First and Town creeks are the weathered remains of the abandoned Bully Hill Mine. You can dock and explore around the mine, but be careful of open pits and tunnels that could collapse.

The smoothest water in the lake is found on the Pit River arm, and that makes it extremely popular with water skiers during the hot months. They are gone by fall, however, and bass fishing takes precedence. The Pit was the only arm of the lake that was not cleared of trees and snags before the lake was flooded. Bass feed and lay their eggs around the snags that were once trees covering the slopes above the fast-flowing Pit River, and the large schools of fish that congregate there make for unsurpassed bass fishing.

The Sacramento River is the largest of the four arms, and a trip up it leads past Digger Bay where you can walk among evidence of Native American burial grounds and fire rings. Across the bay the Dry Fork area has many sheltered coves where you can find peace and solitude any night, and the trout fishing in this area is some of the best in the lake. A mile-long hiking trail leads to the Golinski Mine, a large open pit copper mine, and continues to the top of a ridge that overlooks both Digger Bay and Little Backbone Creek Inlet.

Whatever your desire, you can discover it around Shasta Lake during the off-season. That is, unless you like crowds, loud speed boats and fishing lines tangled by careless waterskiers—for those you have to visit the lake in mid-season. For braying wild burros, undisturbed herons and mother deer with this year's fawns, take a houseboat up the arms of the lake during the fall. You may even get to see some color on the hillsides where oak, maple, redbud and willow near the shoreline of feeder creeks are turning red and yellow before their leaves fall.

The Redding Convention and Visitors Bureau at 777 Auditorium Drive, Redding, CA 96070, will send you a free package of houseboat information upon request.

NOVEMBER

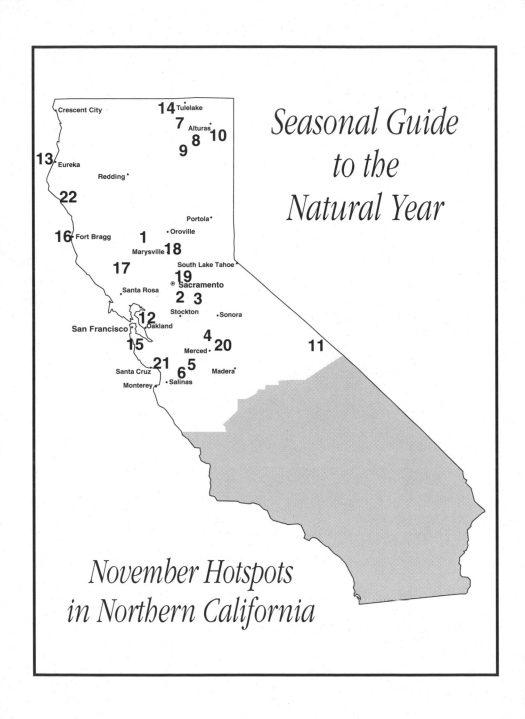

Crescent City

14 Tulelake
7 Alturas
8 10
9

13 Eureka
Redding

22

Portola
16 Fort Bragg   1   Oroville
Marysville 18

17   South Lake Tahoe
19
Santa Rosa   Sacramento
2   3
Stockton
12 Oakland   Sonora
San Francisco
15   4 20
Merced
21 5
6
Santa Cruz   Madera
Monterey   Salinas

11

Seasonal Guide
to the
Natural Year

November Hotspots
in Northern California

MAP SITE KEY

1. Sacramento NWR Complex
2. Consumnes Preserve
3. Woodbridge Road Ecological Preserve
4. George J. Hatfield SRA
5. Merced NWR
6. Los Banos Wildlife Area
7. Lava Beds NM
8. Timber Mountain
9. Ash Creek Wildlife Area
10. Modoc NWR
11. Bishop area
12. San Francisco Bay NWR
13. Eel River Delta
14. Klamath Basin NWR Complex
15. Golden Gate National Recreation Area
16. Jackson State Demonstration Forest
17. Boggs Mountain State Forest
18. Colusa/Sacramento River SRA
19. Folsom Lake SRA
20. McConnell SRA
21. Santa Cruz County
22. Sinkyone Wilderness SP

November Observations

61

Sandhill Cranes

Each fall thousands of stately sandhill cranes descend upon the Central Valley to begin their winter's stay. Nearly thirty thousand of these large gray birds—they stand 3 to 4 feet high—invade the marshes and farmlands in search of winter food. They arrive in small flocks, but gather into large flocks that can number into the thousands after they reach favored roosting sites.

Two subspecies of sandhill cranes, greater and lesser, are found in California. The lesser is by far the most numerous, with over twenty-five thousand returning each winter to feed and rest in the Central Valley from the southwestern coast of Alaska, where they breed. The greater sandhill crane breeds in the northeastern corner of California, but winters along with the lesser in the Central Valley.

Although the greater is somewhat larger, both birds are large, elegant creatures whose gregariousness and strange social activities are reminiscent of human behavior. This is evident both in flight and when they are on the ground. During landings and takeoffs they are very vocal with loud, rattling, buglelike calls that echo across marshes and fields.

While on the ground they dance. One will lower its head while lifting and spreading its wings, then suddenly raise its head, lower its wings, and jump into the air. The birds may also pick up a stick or piece of vegetation and throw it into the air as they jump around. Two birds may begin this dance in synchrony, and others will join in as the movement quickly spreads throughout the flock.

The cranes leave their roosts shortly after sunrise each day to fly to adjacent fields where they will forage until shortly before sundown, and it is during the movement from roost to field and back that you can most appreciate the size and beauty of the cranes.

Sandhill cranes are long-lived (some cranes have lived as long as eighty years in captivity), and they mate for life. They pair off and breed in their third or fourth year, and they maintain contact with their mates throughout the year. Lone birds are frequently seen flying over the roosting flock, calling. This is apparently an attempt to find a lost mate, parent or offspring.

HOTSPOTS

The wetlands of the Central Valley are the roosting areas of choice for the sandhill crane, but as with other large, migratory birds the habitat for the cranes is threatened by development and encroachment by agriculture. While there is no upside to urban development that destroys crane habitat, there is one to agriculture. Cranes forage in the fallow fields and find a more than adequate food supply there during their long winter. The large rice fields that surround the national wildlife refuges and state wildlife management areas are an attraction to the cranes, and they congregate near them.

Cranes can be seen near the large agricultural fields around the refuges in the **Sacramento NWR Complex**. Most are near the Sacramento and Delevan NWRs.

The **Sacramento NWR** is located 5 miles south of Willows off I-5. Take the Norman Road exit and go north along the frontage road for 2 miles to the refuge entrance.

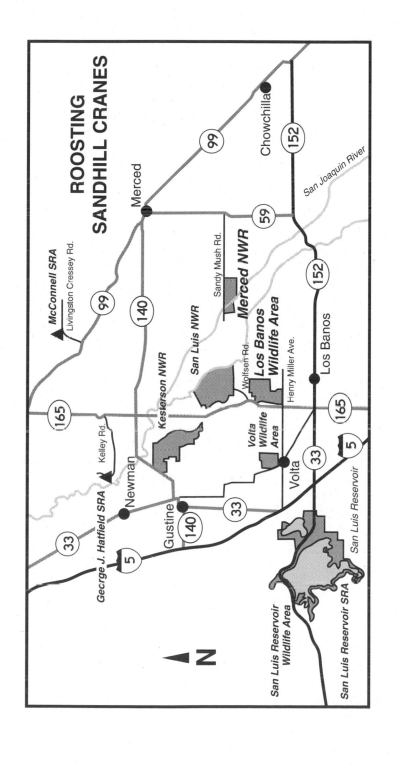

The **Delevan NWR** is also south of Willows. Take the Maxwell exit off I-5 and continue east for 4 miles on Maxwell Road to the refuge.

The Nature Conservancy protects a large sandhill crane habitat area at its **Consumnes River Preserve** off I-5 between Sacramento and Stockton. From I-5 take Twin Cities Road east to Franklin Boulevard and turn south for 1.5 miles to the preserve. You are most likely to see the cranes on the west side of Franklin Boulevard.

The **Woodbridge Road Ecological Preserve** is one of the best places to photograph sandhill cranes. Here the cranes feed in nearby fields and their roosts are clearly visible. Take CA 12 east off I-5 to Thornton Road. Head north on Thornton to Woodbridge. Turn left on Woodbridge and go about 2 miles to the parking area.

The **George J. Hatfield SRA** sits along the Merced River and sandhill crane roost among its fine riparian habitat. Take CA 165 (Lander Avenue) south from CA 99 near Turlock to CR J18. Turn right on CR J18 and continue to Kelley Road. Turn right on Kelley to the park entrance.

Merced NWR offers the best opportunity of all the refuges in the state to see sandhill cranes. Take CA 59 south from Merced to Sandymush Road. Turn west on Sandymush and continue to the refuge entrance.

Sandhill cranes also congregate in large numbers at the **Los Banos Wildlife Area**. The California Department of Fish and Game purchased the first 3,000 acres of this river overflow land in 1929 and made it the first waterfowl refuge in the state. Today there are 5,586 acres in the wildlife area, and birders find it a delightful place to watch for migrating waterfowl and wading birds such as sandhill cranes.

Take CA 165 north from Los Banos for 3 miles. Turn east on Henry Miller Avenue and continue for 1 mile to the refuge.

Those who would like to see the courtship dance of the greater sandhill crane during breeding season can head for the **Ash Creek Wildlife Area** (see Chapter 19) in March and April.

62

Wintering Deer and Pronghorn

During the summer, when higher elevations are free of snow and the browsing is good, deer are seldom seen in the open sagebrush lands of the Modoc Plateau or farther south along the edge of the Great Basin on the eastern slope of the Sierra Nevada. Even the pronghorn, who stay in the sagebrush year-round, move into higher country. To see either species from the time the snow melts in the spring until the first heavy snows fall in the autumn requires considerable effort. During this time the deer stay in small groups that are loosely attached to a larger herd or even as single individuals who only maintain marginal contact with the larger groups.

After the heavy snows of winter begin falling at the higher elevations that isn't the case, however. Does, bucks, yearlings and this year's young all flee the cold winds and deep snow that hides their food supply and collect into large herds at lower elevations. It is then that it is relatively easy to locate both deer and pronghorn.

Both white-tailed and mule deer are found in the northeastern corner of California, but only the mule deer inhabit the area south along the California border toward Mono Lake and Bishop. Pronghorn are found in both regions.

Pronghorn are North America's swiftest animal and can reach speeds of more than 40 miles per hour. They can also cover 20 feet in a single leap—not enough to jump tall buildings, but certainly enough to outdistance most predators.

It is not only the cold of the higher elevations that brings the loosely knit herds together in the fall, but that is also the time of the rut, when bucks vie with each other for the females in the herd. The rutting season is usually over by November, however, and the pregnant females have little contact with any males except this year's young.

HOTSPOTS

The pronghorn and deer congregate in large winter herds at elevations where the snows are light at worst and where the open country provides adequate browse to feed large numbers. Such locations are found along the high country of the Modoc Plateau and along the edge of the Great Basin. Many of these spots are difficult to reach in late fall, but the four below are easily accessible even in the hardest winters.

Lava Beds National Monument is famous for its lava tubes, caves and rugged flows, as well as Captain Jack's Stronghold, where the last major Indian battle in the United States took place near the turn of the century. The remoteness of the monument, the large areas of good browse and the light snowfall all make the monument an excellent spot to view large herds of deer and pronghorn. Some of the most famous photos of giant bucks guarding their does have been taken in early winter at the monument.

Take CA 139 south from Tulelake for 5 miles and then follow the signs to the monument entrance. Herds can be seen from the roads that cross through the monument.

To the west of Lava Beds along U.S. 395 about 30 miles south of the Oregon border is **Timber Mountain**. This large hill is west of U.S. 395, and the turnoff to it is just north of the California inspection station. Park near the top of the hill and creep up to the rim, then peek toward the west for views of herds that number a hundred or more deer.

South of Lava Beds is **Ash Creek Wildlife Area**, and both deer and pronghorn come to this wide valley during the winter to feed. The area lies just north of CA 299 between Bieber and Adin. The southern entrance is 10 miles west of Adin off CA 299.

Nearby is the **Modoc NWR**, and large herds of pronghorn congregate in the open sagebrush country of the refuge in late fall. Follow U.S. 395 south from Alturas to CR 56. Turn east to CR 115 and turn south. Follow the signs to the refuge.

Much farther south there is a winter deer range where some of the largest herds in California congregate. About 10 miles northwest of **Bishop** at the Inyo-Mono county line Old Sherwin Grade and Boundary roads intersect. The herds here are consistently so large that the Department of Fish and Game in Bishop frequently leads public tours of the range.

63

San Francisco Bay National Wildlife Refuge

Two endangered species—the California clapper rail and the salt-marsh harvest mouse—live in the San Francisco Bay NWR among almost one million waterfowl, shorebirds and wading birds during the winter. The rails and mice can be seen only by diligent searches of the clumps of grass that rise above the inflowing water during high tides, but the waterfowl, shorebirds and wading birds can be seen easily on leisurely walks around the refuge.

The San Francisco Bay NWR was the first urban national wildlife refuge, and its 18,000 acres along the southern end of the San Francisco Bay are surrounded on three sides by extensive development. The rich salt marsh and tidelands that have been preserved within the refuge, however, are the year-round home of hundreds of birds species and a stopover for more than 70 percent of all the shorebirds of the Pacific Flyway.

During midwinter the bird population in the refuge peaks at about one million birds. About 700,000 of those are waterfowl, 250,000 are shorebirds and 50,000 are wading birds. Avocets and black-necked stilts are here by the thousands year-round, while marbled godwits, willets, sandpipers and dowitchers leave for short periods to nest farther north before they return to the refuge the rest of the year.

Egrets and herons are also common all year, along with pintail ducks and mallards. The waterfowl population explodes as the fall migration gets underway, and thousands of gadwalls, scaup, shovelers, cinnamon teal and canvasbacks descend upon the open waters of the refuge.

More than 30 miles of marked trails wind along levee tops and lead around ponds in the refuge. By November these ponds are covered with large flocks of ducks, and shorebirds are abundant as they feed in the tidelands.

In a given year as many as 250 species of birds will be sighted in the refuge, and the refuge headquarters has developed an excellent educational and tour program that introduces visitors to the ecology of the region.

The diversity of the wildlife in the refuge is spectacular, even though it does sit amidst heavy urban development. A single handful of the rich, nutrient-laden bay mud can contain over two hundred thousand tiny living creatures, and these are the building blocks of the marine food chain. Larger marine animals and birds feed upon these microscopic creatures, and during low tide the waters roll back to expose mudflats filled with mussels, clams and oysters.

While the bay waters were so polluted twenty-five years ago that the shellfish were considered unfit to eat, today the water is clean enough that shellfish collecting is permitted in some areas of the refuge. This also bodes well for the birds that feed upon the mollusks. Since pollutants concentrate as they move up the food chain, the birds that wintered over at the refuge a quarter of a century ago were susceptible to long-term effects from the chemicals and industrial wastes that were dumped in the bay. Today we do not have to worry about these so much and can enjoy observing the wintering flocks even that much more.

Bring good walking shoes, binoculars and rain gear when you visit the refuge in November and enjoy walking among a million birds and waterfowl. Keep your eyes on the ground if you don't like the blood chase of the hunt, though, for another bird is found in the refuge—one whose main quest in life is to find a lone duck flying in the air, ready for the taking. Peregrine falcons follow the ducks—their favorite food—on their migration along the Pacific Flyway each fall and prey upon them at their wintering sites. So remember, don't look up if you don't want to chance seeing a peregrine swooping at speeds up to 175 miles per hour from high above the marshes to knock a tasty duck from the skies.

Take the Thornton Avenue exit to the east of the Dumbarton Bridge toll plaza. Follow signs 1.5 miles to the refuge entrance.

64

Tundra Swans

Some people say the tundra swan's call is mellow, high-pitched and cooing; others have compared it to soft musical laughter or a clarinet. For the life of me I can't imagine the yelps, howls and barks emanating from these large birds, as they gather in for the night or fight for feeding territory, as being either mellow or musical. It certainly can't be from their call that they got the name "whistling swan," by which the tundra swan is also known.

It is easier to understand where tundra comes from, for these majestic birds migrate north early each spring to the frigid tundra along the coast of Alaska and western Canada, where they depend upon the layers of fat they accumulated during their winter in Northern California to survive their enforced stay on nests during the incubation period. By the time their eggs hatch the weather has warmed, and during the long summer Arctic days the young grow quickly.

When the days begin to cool the tundra swans and the year's cygnets begin the long flight to their wintering grounds in Northern California. There they will settle in to feed on eelgrass and forage in fallow fields.

Tundra swans are large, almost 5 feet from beak to tail with a 7-foot wingspan, and weigh about 20 pounds. Only black legs and bills, plus a small spot of yellow in front of each eye on the bill, mar their pure white coloration.

Tundra swans are one of only two species of swans native to North America. The other is the trumpeter, which was almost annihilated by market hunters in the eighteenth and nineteenth centuries and now survives only in a few locations in the west. Tundra swans were also hunted extensively, but survived the onslaught only to be threatened with a blight that decimated their favorite food supply, eelgrass. They adapted and followed Canada geese into fields near their winter feeding grounds. The new food supply was a salvation for the swans, and their numbers are now at recent highs.

HOTSPOTS

You can see hundreds of the beautiful tundra swans on the **Eel River Delta** just south of Eureka each winter. Christmas Bird Counts often list over fifteen hundred swans, and it is not unusual to see several hundred at a time floating around on the water and feeding.

The delta is 12 miles south of Eureka. Take Hookton Road west from U.S. 101 for 5 miles to the **Table Bluff/Eel River Wildlife Area**. You should be able to spot swans from the parking area, but if you want a real close-up look you can take a boat from either Crab Park or Cock Robin Island on the north side of the delta or Morgan Slough on the south side. The Camp Weott Guide Services ((707) 786-4187) takes individuals and groups on tours for modest prices.

In the other corner of the state over ten thousand tundra swans winter over at the **Klamath Basin NWR Complex**. Although the white swans are truly large birds, they do get lost at times among the tremendous flocks of geese that settle in at the three refuges in the complex.

You can get information about the best spots to see large flocks of swan at the refuge headquarters outside Tulelake. The headquarters is located 5 miles west of

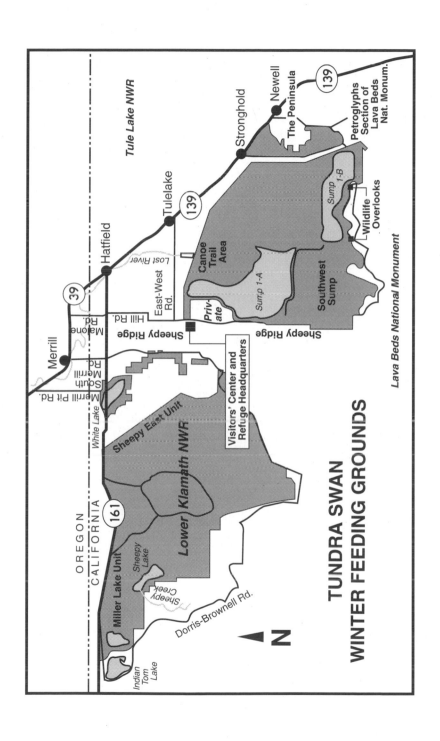

TUNDRA SWAN
WINTER FEEDING GROUNDS

Tulelake on East-West Road, and about .5 mile south on Hill Road.

Flocks of tundra swans that number in the hundreds join the large concentration of sandhill cranes at The Nature Conservancy's **Consumnes River Preserve** between Sacramento and Stockton during early winter. Take the Twin Cities exit off I-5 and head east to Franklin Boulevard. Turn south and continue for 1.5 miles to the preserve entrance.

Closer to Stockton is the **Woodbridge Road Ecological Preserve**, where the swans again join sandhill cranes. The views here are wonderful, and the preserve is easy to reach. Take CA 12 off I-5, and head north on Thornton Road to Woodbridge. Turn left and continue 2 miles to the parking area.

65

November
Shorttakes

FIRST FALL RAINS

After the long, dry summer the first rains in November are a welcome sight. After these fall, it is fun to walk in forests where the dust has been washed from vegetation and the first signs of rejuvenated ferns and mosses appear.

SNOW FALLS AT HIGHER ELEVATIONS

By November the higher peaks of the Sierra generally have been capped with a light pack of snow, and lower slopes may have a dusting. I like to hike along trails in the lower elevations to see if I can spot animal tracks and other signs of the impending winter.

VISIT YOSEMITE

This is also a good time to visit Yosemite. The summer crowds are gone, and the winter ones have yet to appear. While there is little likelihood that there will be snow in the valley, the higher mountains will most likely be covered. You can hike in peace around the valley as you enjoy the sights of Half-Dome and El Capitan with a sprinkling of snow on them.

66

Breakout: Fungus Among Us

Russalas, amanitas, agaricus. Boletes, chanterelles, matsutake. What strange names! Are they carriers of death or haute cuisine? Well, it depends on whether you are fungiphobic or mycologically inclined.

They are mushrooms—fungi fruit. Fruit to fear or salivate over. Or just beautiful objects that spring forth from forest floors after the fall rains begin.

There are several thousand different types of mushrooms found in the western United States, but even the most advanced mycologists seldom are intimately familiar with more than two or three hundred. Some are LBMs (Little Brown Mushrooms) that barely catch the eye of people wandering through forests, while others, such as *Amanita muscaria* (fly amanita) with its cap of red to red-orange with white warts, are so brightly colored they are hard to miss in the muted colors of forest duff. All, however, are a vital part of forest ecology.

Some are parasitic, sponging off living organisms, primarily trees; all others are saprophytic or mycorrhizal. Saprophytic fungi are recyclers. They break down complex organic matter such as wood and humus into simple compounds that replenish the soil of the forest floor.

Fungus thrive in riparian and coastal environments in late fall and early winter.

Mycorrhizal fungi live in mutually beneficial relationships with the tiny rootlets of larger plants, and nutrients are exchanged between the two. Some trees are so dependent upon such fungi that they cannot live without them.

Some mushrooms are tasty morsels that people will literally kill for. The matsutake of the far northwest are so in demand that people are combing national forest land armed with loaded guns to protect themselves against mushroom rustlers who will go to any means to collect this delicacy. The payoff is money—lots of it. Other mushrooms are almost as tasty but more plentiful, therefore not as in demand by commercial gatherers.

Large segments of our population with origins from Japan, Italy, France, Southeast Asia and Russia can't wait for the mushroom season to collect edible delicacies. Others avoid collecting for fear of including a deadly fungi among their catch but still search out unusual fungi for their beauty. If you wish to become one of the former, don't—at least until you have read widely and joined a mycological society where you can learn the fine points of mushroom identification. That will help you avoid the fate of mushroom poisoning, which, while not always deadly, is always painful and distressing.

If you only wish to look, Northern California is one of the best spots in the nation to do so. Its variety of habitats and mild climate make it possible to search for mushrooms almost year-round. Mushrooms prefer temperatures between 40 and 70 degrees Fahrenheit with at least some moisture, and there is some microclimate of the northern part of the state that meets these criteria nearly year-round.

In the High Sierra and southern Cascades the peak season for mushroom hunting is between late July and early September, after the summer thunderstorms, but before the first killing frosts. Lower down in the foothills the season extends from September through November.

It is along the northern California coast and in the Sacramento/San Joaquin Valley that you find mycologists flocking in droves after the first rains begin each fall, generally toward the end of October and the beginning of November. From then until the rains stop in April there is fungus among us.

The most exciting time for collectors, either of photos or the mushrooms themselves, is in November. The rains have come to stay by then and the first burst of fruit has pushed through the forest duff and fallen wood from the mycelia that have been dormant during the dry season. From the redwood forests of the coast to the willow and cottonwood riparian forests of the Central Valley mushrooms appear overnight, only to wither away to be replaced by the next batch.

As with wildflowers, mushrooms have a certain progression. The king bolete fruits early in the season, while you won't see the hedgehog (yes, that is a name for a delectable mushroom generally found on the floor of pine or spruce forests) until much later.

Its takes a real effort to become an expert mycologist, or even an advanced one who can reliably identify edible mushrooms without danger to anyone, but any interested person can enjoy the visual delights offered by the fruits of fungi after the first fall rains.

HOTSPOTS

Head for the woods—any woods. And there you might find mushrooms pushing upward though the mulch of the forest floor. For a more certain outing, though, you can wait for a fall rain and then head to the nearest redwood or riparian forest.

Any of the state parks between Big Sur and the Oregon border along the coast have excellent mushroom displays in late fall and early winter, and so do the protected groves of riparian forests along the rivers between Redding and Fresno in the Central Valley. Be aware that not all of these allow mushroom collecting, however, so check before you attempt to do so. National and state forest lands are normally open to mushroom collecting.

The **Golden Gate National Recreation Area** from Sweeny Ridge to the south of San Francisco to **Point Reyes National Seashore** to the north has long been a collectors' paradise, but several years ago was closed to collecting because so many people were fighting over territory. This may have changed by the time this guide goes to press so check with the recreation area headquarters for current regulations.

The **Jackson State Demonstration Forest** and **Boggs Mountain State Forest** are both good mushrooming sites, and few people venture into them. Jackson State Forest is located inland from Fort Bragg on CA 20. Various dirt roads lead off CA 20 into the midst of the forest. Beware that this may become impassable after heavy rains. You can check with the forest headquarters in Fort Bragg concerning road conditions.

Coast redwoods, Douglas fir and Bishop pine are the dominant trees in the forest, along with tan oak and California bay.

Boggs Mountain State Forest is located a mile north of Cobb in Lake County off Wild Cat Road. This is a mixed conifer and oak forest with an open understory where you should find plenty of mushrooms.

In the Central Valley good collecting sites include the **Colusa/Sacramento River SRA** near downtown Colusa along the river; the **Folsom Lake SRA** near Sacramento where you can look for mushrooms on the oak-covered hills that rise above the lake and the **McConnell SRA** along the Merced River off the Livingston-Cressey Road off CA 99.

Along the central coast you can find mushrooms just about anywhere in **Santa Cruz County**, and mushrooming is so popular in the county that the Santa Cruz City Museum of Natural History offers an annual Fungus Fair later in the season, generally early January.

Farther north along the coast excellent places to hunt for mushrooms in a variety of habitats are located in the **Sinkyone Wilderness SP** and the **Kings Range National Conservation Area**, which extend for miles along the primitive and undeveloped Lost Coast. Any visit to these involves long drives over winding roads and then long, strenuous hikes.

The park and conservation area adjoin along Briceland Road, which heads west from U.S. 101 at Redway. The 36 miles to the coast are curvy and occasionally steep. You can head north into the conservation area from the access point at the coast or south into the park.

DECEMBER

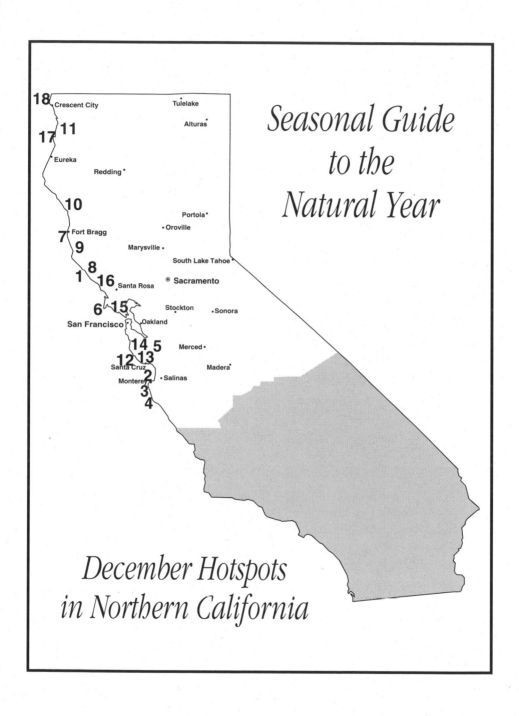

Seasonal Guide
to the
Natural Year

December Hotspots
in Northern California

MAP SITE KEY

1. Dunes Campground—Sonoma Coast State Beaches
2. Natural Bridges State Beach
3. Pacific Grove
4. Point Lobos State Reserve
5. Portola SP
6. Point Reyes National Seashore
7. Van Damme SP
8. Goat Rock—Sonoma Coast State Beaches
9. Mendocino Headlands
10. McKerricher State Beach
11. Humboldt Lagoons SP
12. The Forest of Nisene Marks SP
13. Big Basin Redwoods SP
14. Butano SP
15. Muir Woods National Monument
16. Armstrong Redwoods State Reserve
17. Prairie Creek Redwoods SP
18. Redwood NP

December Observations

67

Monarch
Butterflies

From Sonoma County in the north to Monterey County in the south there are wintering roosts of the colorful monarch butterfly. During the spring and summer months this strikingly beautiful large butterfly is a common sight in fields and gardens across North America as far north as southern Canada. It is one of the most familiar and easily recognized butterflies in the country, which makes it hard to believe that this is a tropical insect—one that is incapable of surviving the harsh winters of most of the nation.

Each fall the insect must withdraw from its summer feeding grounds and head for mild-weather regions. One of these is the central coast of California. Few subfreezing winter storms appear south of Cape Mendocino, and monarchs begin to congregate at one of several dozen winter roosts between Sonoma and Monterey counties in October. By December almost all that are going to winter over have found their roost. These are generally located at the same site winter after winter, for only selected sites meet the demanding requirements of the monarchs.

What is most unusual is that the monarchs that congregate at the roosts each year aren't the ones who left it the previous spring. The journey to the special roosts is made only once by individual monarchs—they do not live to make it a second time. Instead, it is several generations later who survive to navigate across thousands of miles to locate a preferred winter roosting site.

An estimated one hundred million monarchs winter over from October to March in about one hundred roosting sites along the Pacific Coast between Sonoma County and Baja California and a handful in several isolated canyons in Mexico. Monarchs that summer west of the Rockies head for the sites along the coast of California and Baja California. Those that summer east of the Rockies head for central Mexico.

The monarchs begin mating in January, and by March the colonies of young monarchs leave for their spring and summer regions. There they lay their eggs and die within a few weeks. During the spring and summer several generations live and die before the fall migration begins, and the cycle is repeated.

The most well-known roosting site in Northern California is the one in George Washington Park in Pacific Grove on the Monterey Peninsula. Pacific Grove labels itself as "Butterfly Town, USA" and holds an annual parade to mark the return of the monarchs in the fall.

While the monarchs begin to return in October, the largest congregations are seen during December. During the warm spells that frequently grace the central coast during this month the monarchs are more active. On bright days their colors glitter in the winter sun, and they add festive color to winter.

HOTSPOTS

The most popular monarch roosting sites in Northern California are well marked, directions to them are easy and plenty of people visit them each year. Those at the **Dunes Campgrounds** of the **Sonoma Coast State Beaches** just north of Bodega Bay along CA 1 are little visited, however, for the rangers are reluctant to give directions to the coast lupine bushes where the butterflies return each year. In fact, they sometimes refuse even to discuss the fact that a roost exists within the park.

This adds a touch of excitement to the search for the little-known roost. As you enter the campground and day-use area about 3 miles north of Bodega Bay, ask the rangers about the location of the roost. You will probably be met with a blank look and a noncommittal answer, so you should continue to the day-use parking area near the boardwalk to the beach. From there, head south among the bush-lupine covered dunes. Use a grid pattern to search the dunes, looking for the groups of lupines that are covered with orange leaves that flutter gently in the winter breezes. These leaves are monarch butterflies, and when you discover them please be careful to leave them undisturbed. Smoking around the roost or collecting butterflies are both harmful to the colony. Look, take pictures and leave the colony as you found it.

Natural Bridges State Beach along CA 1 near Santa Cruz is more forthcoming about the monarch colonies that roost there each winter. They have marked trails and guided tours where rangers and docents lead you directly to the colonies and explain the life cycle of the monarch in detail. While not as challenging as finding the colonies at Sonoma State Beaches, the colonies at Natural Bridges are a sure thing. You know you will see the monarchs, and you won't have to hike over dunes to do so.

A little farther south in **Pacific Grove** are the famous monarch trees in **George Washington Park** near Point Pinos. Most photographs of monarch colonies come from these trees, and they are right along the street a short walk from the parking lot. Take Central Lighthouse Road from Monterey to its end at George Washington Park in Pacific Grove.

Each year several colonies of monarchs come to **Point Lobos State Reserve** for the winter. The location of the sites here varies from year to year, so the best suggestion is to check with the rangers at the park entrance to find out the location of the current year's colonies.

Point Lobos is located along CA 1, 3 miles south of Carmel.

68

Christmas Bird Count

Each year over fifty thousand birders participate in the National Audubon Society's Christmas Bird Count (universally known among birders as the CBC). This tradition began on Christmas Day, 1900, as ornithologist Frank Chapman and about two dozen friends scattered across the Northeast to see how many birds they could "bag," or count. This was in contrast to the tradition of hunters of that era teaming up on Christmas Day for hunts where they competed for the biggest bag of dead birds.

That begat the Christmas Bird Count, which today occurs during the last two weeks of December and first week of January each year in all states and provinces of the United States and Canada. Counts also take place in other locations around the world.

There are now some sixteen hundred sites in North America, each encompassing a circle 15 miles wide. For a twenty-four-hour period the circle is covered by hundreds of birders who count each and every bird they see. These are then tallied by number of individual birds and number of species represented. Some years almost two hundred million birds are seen in North America during the CBC. Almost forty of the sites are located in Northern

California, including some with the highest counts in the nation.

All work on the CBC is done by volunteers, from organizing the count to the actual counting. Each site is divided into manageable sections where experienced and inexperienced volunteers can work together to ensure even coverage of the area. Some participants begin the count in the early morning hours long before dawn as they call owls near backroads and wooded park areas. Others begin later to catch early morning feeding activity. All go until dark in their quest for high counts of individuals and species.

Although not directly competitive, CBCs around the country do strive for high counts and for the best lists of rare birds. And all look forward each year to the publication of CBC results around their state and the rest of the country. These fill a telephone directory–sized volume crammed with facts and figures.

Volunteers and local Audubon groups are not the only ones interested in the yearly counts. The CBC is the longest continuous survey of winter bird populations in the country, and scientists scour the publications for information on the status of bird populations. These are often used as indicators of the health of the environment.

Honestly, though, most of the volunteers don't venture out into the winter elements for science. Rather, they do it for fun and a chance to meet friends, watch for birds and the traditional compilation dinner where all the volunteers for each site join together for a potluck dinner while their sightings are recorded.

As they down hot drinks and warm food they exclaim about unexpected discoveries and bemoan the lack of one or more species that they normally see.

HOTSPOTS

There are so many great birding sites in northern California that I would be hard pressed to name a "hotspot" that would surpass any of a dozen or so others. And with almost forty sites to choose from each Christmas, there is bound to be a site close to anyone who wishes to volunteer.

Most count leaders—and each Audubon chapter in Northern California has one—welcome new, enthusiastic volunteers whether they are experienced birders or not. You can contact your local Audubon group for the name of the CBC coordinator, the Western Regional Office, 555 Audubon Place, Sacramento, CA 95825; (916) 444-5557, for a list of all sites in the western region, or you can contact the Christmas Bird Count Editor, *American Birds,* National Audubon Society, 700 Broadway, New York, NY, 10003; (212) 979-3000, for a list of counts and compilers in any area for which you are interested in volunteering.

There is a small fee for participating to cover the costs of printing the annual report. Be prepared to stay outdoors all day regardless of weather. CBCers are noted for their lack of regard for inclement weather in their pursuit of a comprehensive bird count of their area.

Be honest about your birding abilities when you contact the site coordinator. If you lack experience you will be teamed with an experienced birder, which will give you an opportunity to learn more about bird identification. There is even an opportunity for those who don't want to brave the elements and would rather have the comfort of home. You can sign up as a feeder watcher, and participate while staying warm.

69

Fern Canyons of the Redwoods

Redwood forests are home to a dozen species of ferns, from the small goldenback fern, which reaches at the most 4 inches in height, to the western chain fern, which can reach 6 feet. These all like the cool, moist microclimate found along creeks and swampy areas deep in redwood forests. There they thrive during the wet season, which lasts from November through April.

During the dry season the ferns become brittle and seem less than happy. It is a time for renewal for ferns—as well as for much of the other undergrowth in the forests—when the first rains fall, and the creeks begin to fill after the wet season begins. The ferns become lush with new moisture, and their green fronds become strong and pliable.

Along streams you will find western chain, five-finger, deer and sword fern. These are all water-loving ferns that give shade to the stream banks.

It's easy to find ferns in redwood country. All you have to do is take a hike in the woods. Ferns are so ubiquitous there that just about every state and national park in the region has either a Fern Canyon or Fern Trail.

Ferns come out in lush growth after the first winter rains.

HOTSPOTS

Portola SP sits in the Santa Cruz Mountains off CA 35 south and east of Half Moon Bay. The 2,400-acre park has 14 miles of hiking trails that lead through fir and redwood forests. The many creeks in the park form steep canyons where ferns become lush and green after the winter rains begin.

Take Alpine Road west off CA 35 for about 3 miles to Portola State Park Road. Turn left and continue to the park entrance after about 3 more miles.

In the southern end of **Point Reyes National Seashore**, **Fern Canyon** is a magical place where ferns cover the floor of a small creek that cuts a canyon through a flat marine terrace. The flat floor of the canyon is a fern-lovers paradise.

To reach Fern Canyon take a left at the north end of Bolinas Lagoon, then take the Olema-Bolinas Road south a

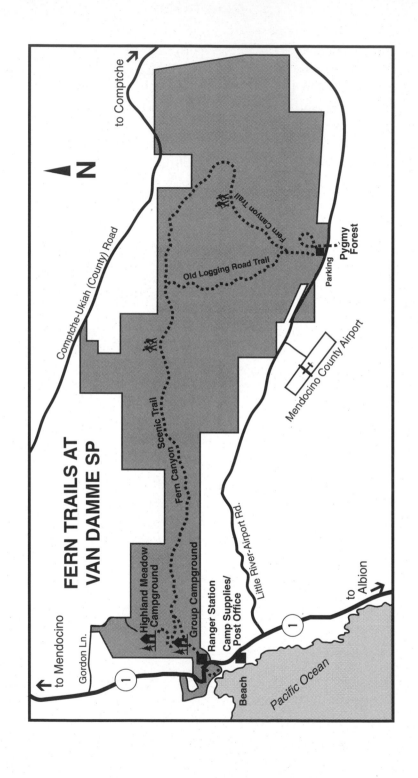

FERN TRAILS AT VAN DAMME SP

N

to Comptche

to Mendocino

to Albion

Comptche-Ukiah (County) Road

Gordon Ln.

Highland Meadow Campground

Group Campground

Ranger Station

Camp Supplies/ Post Office

Beach

Pacific Ocean

Little River-Airport Rd.

Mendocino County Airport

Scenic Trail

Fern Canyon

Old Logging Road Trail

Fern Canyon Trail

Parking

Pygmy Forest

1

little over a mile to Mesa Road. Turn west on Mesa, continue for 4 miles past the Coast Guard Station and park in the parking lot just beyond the Palomarin Field Station of the Point Reyes Bird Observatory. The trail to the canyon begins behind the station.

The primary trail in **Van Damme SP** is the **Fern Canyon Trail**, which bisects the floor of the park and leads 5 miles up the banks of the Little River. Both sides of the canyon are covered with thick growths of ferns, and the easy trail allows you to examine the many different kinds of ferns found there.

Van Damme SP is located along CA 1 about 2 miles south of the village of Mendocino, and you can park in the parking lot for day use, or stay in one of two campgrounds in the park.

Farther north you can find luscious growths of ferns in any of the state and national redwood parks. From Eureka and Crescent City you can reach any of a dozen parks within thirty minutes, and all have easy trails that lead through fern canyons.

70

Winter Storm Beaches

Each summer the slow waves of the Pacific gently deposit sand along the shoreline and extend beaches far beyond where they were in the spring. As summer turns to fall and fall to winter, these flat beaches are swept away by the increasingly larger waves. These are the forewarnings of the winter storms gathering strength far out in the Pacific, but which will soon pound the coast with furious waves.

By December storm activity has generally increased to the point where the beaches are no longer wide, flat stretches of sand. Instead, they drop off precipitously into the surf. The wide beaches of summer have been moved offshore onto shelves where the incoming waves break, pound into the steeper beaches and move even more sand out with the pull of their undertow.

Winter is a wild time on Northern California beaches. Driftwood rushes out of the mouth of the roaring rivers and is swept southward along the coast by the tides. It soon returns to land on beaches that jut out into the ocean. California gulls have returned from their summer breeding grounds inland with this year's fledglings, and all squabble as they scrounge through the debris being deposited on the beaches. Ominous clouds replace hovering fog offshore, and winds whip up the waves to warn of incoming storms.

As the storms hit the beaches the waves rise. No longer are they slow breakers that gently run up the beach. Now they *whump* against shore and cliffs with a power that sends cold spray hundreds of feet skyward. Anything in the way gets moved without care.

The power of these waves is overwhelming even along the flattest stretches of beach, but it is unimaginable as they pound against seastacks and cliffs along the more rugged sections of the coast. There, 15- and 20-foot waves rise upward of 50 feet as following waves push the foam and froth ever higher until gravity pulls the tower of water back to earth into the breaking waves below.

The power of these actions becomes stronger as you head north along the coast. What are mild storms along the Sonoma Coast are raging ones as you reach the Humboldt and Del Norte coasts. They are all, however, an exciting display of nature's raw power and well worth venturing out to see at their peak. When the full fury of the storms' wind and rain hit the coast most people retire to the warmth and comfort of their cozy homes.

Others—seen as less than sane by those who seek the comfort of home and hearth—go forth to experience nature at its most furious, much as John Muir did when he tied himself to the top of a sugar pine during a Sierra storm. Visiting a stormy beach is much less dangerous, but you get just as invigorating an experience.

HOTSPOTS

With large seastacks just offshore, a long beach and the mouth of the Russian River nearby, **Goat Rock** in the **Sonoma Coast State Beaches** offers breaking waves, piles of driftwood and exposed beaches where you can feel the powerful forces of the winds as they come off the ocean.

The Sonoma Coast State Beaches extend 13 miles along CA 1 from Bodega Bay north to Jenner and the mouth of the Russian River, where Goat Rock is located.

Mendocino Headlands jut out into the Pacific Ocean in the village of Mendocino, and you can get wonderful views of waves breaking against seacliffs and seastacks both to the north and south. Coves channel the power of the waves as they break over small rock islands, and waves spray high into the air where the storm winds push their salty mist ashore. Even in the midst of rainstorms you can taste and smell the salt from the sea. The park lies seaward of the village of Mendocino off CA 1.

At **McKerricher State Beach** you can stand far above the waves breaking against tall seacliffs to watch the power of winter storms, but don't get too careless. Rogue waves have been known to reach above the 50-foot-high cliffs to sweep unsuspecting watchers out into the sea. Keep an eye out for incoming waves that appear larger than the ones before and after and move away from the cliff's edge to avoid that fate.

There is also a wide expanse of beach here where driftwood washes ashore during the winter storms. The park entrance is off CA 1 three miles north of Fort Bragg.

Humboldt Lagoons SP/Harry A. Merlo SRA is made up of three lagoons that lie along the coast 31 miles north of Eureka off U.S. 101. Two of them, **Big Lagoon** and **Stone Lagoon**, frequently fill to capacity and overflow into the ocean during heavy winter storms. When they do they carve deep channels into the sandy beach, and their water level drops as much as 6 feet per hour. Later storms rebuild the sand dams that hold the waters of the lagoon. The lagoon refills, only to overflow once again in the next really big storm.

This area is one where the power of the ocean is felt year-round, and incoming winter storms thrash the

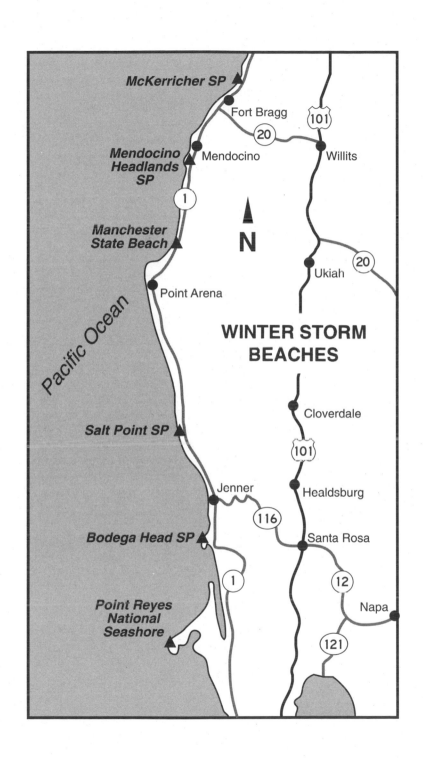

McKerricher SP

Fort Bragg

101

20

Willits

Mendocino
Headlands
SP

Mendocino

1

Manchester
State Beach

20

Ukiah

Point Arena

Pacific Ocean

**WINTER STORM
BEACHES**

Cloverdale

101

Salt Point SP

Jenner

Healdsburg

116

Bodega Head SP

Santa Rosa

1

12

Point Reyes
National
Seashore

Napa

121

N

beaches with furious blasts of rain and wind. The beaches are no place for the timid or meek as the waves reach high on the beaches, the lagoons fill with water that churns from the gale force winds and the rain pelts anything that is exposed.

71

December
Shorttakes

FIRST SNOW TRIPS

Almost always this is the time to make your first snow trip. A good pack is on the ground, but maybe not enough to bring out all the skiers. You can toboggan or sled in areas where you are not able to go later in the season, and the snow has yet to turn to the hard icy surface that comes with repeated cold and warm periods.

CHRISTMAS TREE CUTTING

While urban residents have to buy their trees from the corner lot most people in Northern California have the opportunity to cut their own tree each year. This can be either at a tree farm (and there are dozens in the Sierra foothills and to the north and south of San Francisco along the coast) or in one of the national forests in the region. For the national forests, you have to obtain a permit from the local ranger district, and some districts may prohibit any cutting.

TULE FOG

The first big tule fogs of the year generally appear in the Central Valley during December. Tule fogs are formed when evaporation from the soaked ground rises to meet cold winter air. The name came from the common occurrence of these fogs around tule-covered wetlands. These fogs are known for the danger they cause on the heavily traveled freeways of the Central Valley, but this is also an interesting time to explore park lands to see how the wildlife adjusts to the fogs.

72

Breakout: Banana Slugs

Banana slugs are slimy. They are also big—and revolting to many people who encounter them the first time. Others, however, see them as one of the most fascinating creatures found in the redwood forests that rise above slopes near the coast all the way from Big Sur in the south to the Oregon border.

Students at the University of California–Santa Cruz have even chosen the banana slug as their school mascot, and the city of Guerneville along the Russian River had a Banana Slug Festival for many years before local celebrities and politicians tired of eating culinary concoctions that featured banana slugs as the primary ingredient.

This large soft-bodied mollusk is superbly adapted for living in the wet undergrowth of the redwood forests where it thrives on leafy and decaying vegetation. While slugs in many areas come out only at night or during damp days, those in the redwoods feed during most days of the wet season. This is especially so after the first rains of winter have fallen, and the olive-colored banana slug can be readily seen as it slowly moves over fallen debris in search of delicacies. They tend toward yellow in color and often have darker olive spots on their backs. Some reach over 6 inches in

Banana slug in search of food on an old redwood log.

length and can stretch even longer as they move. You can spot where the slugs have traveled by the slimy track they leave as they move across the vegetation.

December is an excellent time to look for banana slugs in redwood forests since the early rains have provided the moisture necessary to bring the slugs out during the day. The hard cold that sometimes comes in January and February and keeps the slugs from moving around is still ahead.

HOTSPOTS

Hikers rule **The Forest of Nisene Marks SP**, for there is limited auto access. You can drive along a dirt road to the picnic areas, but trails lead you into the steep canyons where six creeks originate. With elevations ranging from 190 to 2,600 feet, the park offers challenging hikes to even the most jaded walkers. Over 90 percent of the park is covered with dense forests, and this is the preferred habitat of the banana slug.

From CA 1 east of Santa Cruz take the Aptos-Seacliff exit and turn north on Aptos Creek Road. Continue to the park parking area.

Big Basin Redwoods SP is California's oldest state park and has one of the best old-growth forests in the state. The tallest redwood in the park measures 329 feet high. Most visitors take the .6-mile-long trail that leads through the principal grove in the park, and you should see plenty of banana slugs there. Longer, more strenuous trails lead you into the interior of the redwood groves where slugs adorn most piles of debris.

Take CA 9 north from Santa Cruz to Boulder Creek for 13 miles and then take CA 236 9 miles to the park, or from Cupertino take CA 85 off I-280 and go 6 miles to Saratoga. Turn right on CA 9 and head 7 miles to Saratoga Gap. From there take CA 236 14 miles to Big Basin.

Butano SP is another primarily hiking park, although it does have campgrounds. About 80 percent of the park is covered with forests, and its location near the ocean means very wet winters. Look for slugs among the undergrowth during warm days.

Take CA 1 15 miles south of Half Moon Bay and turn inland on Pescadero Road. After 2 miles turn south on Cloverdale Road at the small town of Pescadero and go 5 miles to the park entrance.

Muir Woods National Monument, part of the extensive Golden Gate National Recreation Area, is one of the most visited redwood groves in the state. That does not make it any less worthy, however, as a site to see banana slugs. They abound among the undergrowth near the creeks, and as you reach the upper ends of the canyon you can leave the paved trails to get an up-close look at them.

Take the Stinson Beach exit off U.S. 101 just past Sausalito and follow the signs to Muir Woods. Beware, the road is narrow, curvy and not for the faint of heart. Visitors from the east and midwest are particularly dismayed at traveling over it.

Armstrong Redwoods State Reserve, another popular first- and second-growth grove, has plenty of easy trails where you can walk through the understory of a tall redwood grove. Look for slugs all along the way.

Take CA 116 off U.S. 101 at Cotati and head west for 16 miles to Guerneville on the Russian River. From the four-way stop in Guerneville go straight for another 2 miles to the park entrance. Park outside the gate and walk into the heart of the grove.

Prairie Creek Redwoods SP parallels U.S. 101 for 8 miles about 50 miles north of Eureka. This park has just about everything you will find in the redwoods, including large numbers of banana slugs.

Redwood NP has everything Prairie Creek does, except more and bigger. Redwood NP, Jedediah Smith Redwoods SP, Prairie Creek Redwoods SP and Del Norte Coast Redwoods SP are contiguous and include the largest groves, as well as the largest trees, of old growth redwoods in California. They extend along both sides of U.S. 101 between Orick and Crescent City.

```
┌─────────────────┐
└─────────────────┘
```

APPENDIX

Following is a list of addresses and phone numbers for wildlife refuges, parks, preserves and organizations. The ones mentioned in the text are included along with others that may be of interest. Only those preserves and refuges open to the public are listed.

FEDERAL AGENCIES

National Parks

National Park Service
Western Regional Office
Building 201, Fort Mason
San Francisco, CA 94123
(415) 556-0560

Devils Postpile National Monument
P.O. Box 501
Mammoth Lakes, CA 93546
(619) 934-2289

Golden Gate National Recreation Area
Building 201, Fort Mason
San Francisco, CA 94123
(415) 556-0560

Lassen Volcanic National Park
38050 Hwy 36 E
P.O. Box 100
Mineral, CA 96063
(916) 595-4444

Lava Beds National Monument
P.O. Box 867
Tulelake, CA 96134
(916) 667-2282

Pinnacles National Monument
Paicines, CA 95043
(408) 389-4485

Point Reyes National Seashore
Point Reyes Station, Ca 94956
(415) 663-1092

Redwood National Park
1111 Second Street
Crescent City, CA 95531
(707) 464-6101

Whiskeytown-Shasta-Trinity National Recreation Area
P.O. Box 188
Whiskeytown, CA 96095
(916) 241-6584

Yosemite National Park
P.O. Box 577
Yosemite National Park, CA 95389
(209) 372-0200

National Forests

U.S. Forest Service
Pacific Southwest Region
630 Sansome Street
San Francisco, CA 94111
(415) 705-2874

Almanor Ranger District
900 East Hwy 36, P.O. Box 767
Chester, CA 96020
(916) 258-2141

Amador Ranger District
26820 Silver Drive
Star Route 3
Pioneer, CA 95666
(209) 295-4251

Beckwourth Ranger District/Mohawk Ranger Station
Mohawk Road, P.O. Box 7
Blairsden, CA 96013
(916) 836-2575

Big Bar Ranger District
Star Route 1, Box 10
Big Bar, CA 96010
(916) 623-6106

Big Valley Ranger District
P.O. Box 159
Adin, CA 96006
(916) 299-3215

Bridgeport Ranger District
P.O. Box 595
Bridgeport, CA 93517
(619) 932-7070

Calaveras Ranger District
Hwy 4, P.O. Box 500
Hathaway Pines, CA 95233
(209) 795-1381

Corning Ranger District
22000 Corning Road
P.O. Box 1019
Corning, CA 96021
(916) 824-5196

Covelo Ranger District
Route 1, Box 62-C
Covelo, CA 95428
(707) 983-6118

Devil's Garden Ranger District
P.O. Box 5
Canby, CA 96015
(916) 233-4611

Doublehead Ranger District
P.O. Box 369
Tulelake, CA 96134
(916) 667-2247

Downieville Ranger District
15924 Hwy 49
Camptonville, CA 95922
(916) 288-3231

Eagle Lake Ranger District
c/o USFS
55 South Sacramento Street
Susanville, CA 96130
(916) 257-2151

El Dorado National Forest Information Center
3070 Camino Heights Drive
Camino, CA 95709
(916) 644-6048

El Dorado National Forest Superintendent
100 Forni Road
Placerville, CA 95667
(916) 622-5061

Foresthill Ranger District
22830 Auburn-Foresthill Road
Foresthill, CA 95631
(916) 367-2224

Gasquet Ranger District
P.O. Box 228
Gasquet, CA 95543
(707) 457-3131

Georgetown Ranger District
7600 Wentworth Springs Road
Georgetown, CA 95634
(916) 333-4312

Goosenest Ranger District
37805 Hwy 97
Macdowel, CA 96058
(916) 398-4391

Greenville Ranger District
410 Main Street
P.O. Box 329
Greenville, CA 95947
(916) 284-7126

Groveland Ranger District
Hwy 120-Star Route, P.O. Box 75 G
Groveland, CA 95321
(209) 962-7825

Happy Camp Ranger District
Hwy 96, P.O. Box 377
Happy Camp, CA 96039
(916) 493-2243

Hat Creek Ranger District
P.O. Box 220
Fall River Mills, CA 96028
(916) 336-5521

Hayfork Ranger District
P.O. Box 159
Hayfork, CA 96041
(916) 628-5227

Inyo National Forest Superintendent
873 N. Main Street
Bishop, CA 93514
(619) 873-5841

Klamath National Forest Superintendent
1312 Fairlane Road
Yreka, CA 96097
(916) 842-6131

Lake Tahoe Basin Management Unit
870 Emerald Bay Road, Suite 1
South Lake Tahoe, CA 96150
(916) 573-2600

LaPorte Ranger District/Challenge Ranger Station
10087 LaPorte Road
P.O. Drawer 369
Challenge, CA 95925
(916) 675-2462

Lassen National Forest Superintendent
55 South Sacramento Street
Susanville, CA 96130
(916) 257-2151

Lower Trinity Ranger District
P.O. Box 668
Willow Creek, CA 95573
(916) 629-2118

Mad River Ranger District
Star Route, Box 300
Bridgeville, CA 95526
(707) 574-6233

Mammoth Ranger District
P.O. Box 148
Mammoth Lakes, CA 93546
(619) 924-5500

McCloud Ranger District
P.O. Box 1620
McCloud, CA 96057
(916) 964-2184

Mendocino National Forest Superintendent
420 East Laurel Street
Willows, CA 95988
(916) 934-3316

Milford Ranger District/Laufman Ranger Station
Milford, CA 96121
(916) 253-2223

Mi-Wok Ranger District
Hwy 108E, P.O. Box 100
Mi-Wok Village, CA 95346
(209) 965-3434

Modoc National Forest Superintendent
441 North Main Street
Alturas, CA 96101
(916) 233-5811

Mono Lake Ranger District
P.O. Box 429
Lee Vining, CA 93541
(619) 647-6525

Mt. Shasta Ranger District
204 West Alma
Mt. Shasta, CA 96067
(916) 926-4511

Nevada City Ranger District
631 Coyote St.
P.O. Box 6003
Nevada City, CA 95959-6003
(916) 265-4538

Oak Knoll Ranger District
22541 Hwy 96
Klamath River, CA 96050
(916) 465-2241

Orleans Ranger District
Drawer B
Orleans, CA 95556
(916) 627-3291

Oroville Ranger District
875 Mitchell Avenue
Oroville, CA 95965
(916) 534-6500

Pacific Ranger District
Pollock Pines, CA 95726
(916) 644-2349

Placerville Ranger District
3491 Carson Court
Placerville, CA 95667
(916) 644-2324

Plumas National Forest Superintendent
159 Lawrence Street
P.O. Box 11500
Quincy, CA 95971
(916) 283-2050

Quincy Ranger District
39696 Hwy 70
Quincy, CA 95971
(916) 283-0555

Salmon River Ranger District
Hwy 36, P.O. Box 280
Etna, CA 96027
(916) 467-5757

Scott River Ranger District
11263 North Hwy 3
Fort Jones, CA 96032
(916) 468-5351

Shasta Lake Ranger District
14225 Holiday Road
Redding, CA 96003
(916) 275-1587

Shasta-Trinity National Forest Superintendent
2400 Washington Avenue
Redding, CA 93257
(916) 246-5222

Sierraville Ranger District
P.O. Box 95
Sierraville, CA 96126
(916) 994-3401

Six Rivers National Forest Superintendent
500 5th Street
Yreka, CA 95501
(707) 442-1721

Stanislaus National Forest Superintendent
19777 Greenley Road
Sonora, CA 95370
(209) 532-3671

Stonyford Ranger District
Stites Ladoga Road
Stonyford, CA 95979
(916) 963-3128

Tahoe National Forest Superintendent
631 Coyote Street
P.O. Box 6063
Nevada City, CA 95959
(916) 265-4531

Toiyabe National Forest Superintendent
1200 Franklin Way
Sparks, NV 89431
(702) 331-6444

Truckee Ranger District
P.O. Box 909
Truckee, CA 95734
(916) 587-3558

Ukonom Ranger District
P.O. Drawer 410
Orleans, CA 95556
(916) 627-3291

Upper Lake Ranger District
Middlecreek Road, P.O. Box 96
Upper Lake, CA 95485
(707) 275-2361

Warner Mountain Ranger District
P.O. Box 220
Cedarville, CA 96104
(916) 279-6116

Weaverville Ranger District
P.O. Box 1190
Weaverville, CA 96093
(916) 623-2131

White Mountain Ranger District
798 N. Main Street
Bishop, CA 93514
(619) 873-2525

Yolla Bolla Ranger District
Platina, CA 96076
(916) 352-4211

Bureau of Land Management

BLM California State Office
2800 Cottage Way, E-2807
Sacramento, CA 95825
(916) 978-4754

Alturas Resource Area
608 West 12th Street
Alturas, CA 96101
(916) 233-4666

Arcata Resource Area
1125 16th Street, Room 219
P.O. Box 1112
Arcata, CA 95521
(707) 822-7648

Bakersfield District Office
Federal Office Building, Room 311
800 Truxton Avenue
Bakersfield, CA 93301
(805) 861-4191

Bishop Resource Area
787 North Main Street, Suite P
Bishop, CA 93514
(619) 872-4881

Clear Lake Resource Area
555 Leslie Street
Ukiah, CA 95482
(707) 462-3873

Eagle Lake Resource Area
2454 Riverside Drive
Susanville, CA 96130
(916) 257-0456

Folsom Resource Area
63 Natoma Street
Folsom, CA 95630
(916) 985-4474

Hollister Resource Area
P.O. Box 365
Hollister, CA 95024
(408) 637-8183

Redding Resource Area
355 Hemsted Drive
Redding, CA 96002
(916) 246-5325

Surprise Resource Area
602 Cressler Street
Cedarville, CA 96104
(916) 279-6101

Susanville District Office
705 Hall Street
Susanville, CA 96130
(916) 257-5381

Ukiah District Office
555 Leslie Street
Ukiah, CA 95482
(707) 462-3873

National Wildlife Refuges

Castle Rock NWR
c/o Humboldt Bay NWR
Route 1, Box 76
Loleta, CA 95551
(707) 733-5406
Castle Rock is an island near Crescent City with the second
largest seabird breeding colony in California. Located a half-
mile offshore, it is not open to the public, but birds can be
observed from the mainland or by boat offshore.

Clear Lake NWR
c/o Klamath Basin NWR Complex
Route 1, Box 74
Tulelake, CA 96134
(916) 667-2231
A large refuge located about 15 miles southeast of Tulelake. Closed to the public from spring to early fall to protect nesting birds such as pelicans and cormorants. Some nesting sites are visible from outside the refuge boundaries.

Coleman National Fish Hatchery
Route 1, Box 2105
Anderson, CA 96007
(916) 365-8622
This hatchery is located on Battle Creek about a mile from the Sacramento River. It hatches chinook and steelhead salmon that migrate up the Sacramento River from the Pacific Ocean.

Colusa NWR
c/o Sacramento NWR Complex
Route 1, Box 311
Willows, CA 95988
(916) 934-2801
Just west of Colusa on CA 20, this refuge has waterfowl present from September through March, with the peak periods for observations in December and January.

Delevan NWR
c/o Sacramento NWR Complex
Route 1, Box 311
Willows, CA 95988
(916) 934-2801
Although this refuge is closed to public access you can view the large flocks of ducks and geese that congregate here in

the winter from Four Mile Road which parallels the western boundary of the refuge.

Farallon NWR
c/o San Francisco Bay NWR
P.O. Box 524
Newark, CA 94560-0524
(510) 792-0222
The largest seabird breeding colony on the Pacific Coast south of Alaska is located on these islands 26 miles off the Golden Gate. Although the refuge is closed to visitors, a number of conservation groups sponsor wildlife observation trips each year. Information about these is available at the San Francisco Bay NWR visitors' center.

Humboldt Bay NWR
Route 1, Box 76
Loleta, CA 95551
(707) 733-5406
The refuge has tracts on both ends of Humboldt Bay. The area is an important staging area, especially in the spring, for the Pacific black brant and other migratory waterfowl.

Kesterson NWR
c/o San Luis NWR Complex
340 "I" Street
P.O. Box 2176
Los Banos, CA 93635
(209) 826-3508
This refuge became notorious for the selenium deposits left from agricultural runoff. These caused birth defects in some birds hatched in the refuge, but attempts are being made to solve the problem. Vernal pools in the refuge are some of the best in the state.

Lower Klamath NWR
c/o Klamath Basin NWR Complex
Route 1, Box 74
Tulelake, CA 96134
(916) 667-2231
One of several refuges in the complex that lies along the Oregon border. The largest concentration of bald eagles in the lower forty-eight states, as well as over a million waterfowl, collects here in the winter.

Merced NWR
c/o San Luis NWR Complex
340 "I" Street
P.O. Box 2176
Los Banos, CA 93635
(209) 826-3508
Great area for viewing sandhill cranes in winter, along with many waterfowl.

Modoc NWR
P.O. Box 1610
Alturas, CA 96101
(916) 233-3572
Waterfowl, including tundra swans, are numerous in winter. Greater sandhill cranes nest here in spring, and white pelicans are plentiful in summer. Deer and pronghorn live here year-round.

Red Bluff Diversion Dam Salmon Viewing Plaza
Sale Lane
Red Bluff, CA 96080
(916) 527-3043
Located on the east bank of the Sacramento downstream from Red Bluff, this viewing plaza is open daily from April through November from 6:00 A.M. to 8:00 P.M.

Sacramento NWR
Route 1, Box 311
Willows, CA 95988
(916) 934-2801
Although waterfowl are present from September through
March, the peak viewing times are November through January
when over a million ducks and geese stop over to feed.

Sacramento River NWR
Route 1, Box 311
Willows, CA 95988
(916) 934-2801
This refuge has limited public access, but you can canoe
along its boundaries on the Sacramento River. Call for the
latest information about acquisitions and access.

Salinas River NWR
c/o San Francisco Bay NWR Complex
P.O. Box 524
Newark, CA 94560-0524
(510) 792-0222
Located at the confluence of the Salinas River and Monterey
Bay, this refuge offers varied habitat for a wide variety of
birds, including the rare snowy plover and the endangered
brown pelican and peregrine falcon.

San Francisco Bay NWR
1 Marshland Road
Fremont, CA 94536
Mailing address:
P.O. Box 524
Newark, CA 94560-0524
(510) 792-0222
A large refuge with an excellent visitors' center, environmen-
tal education program and good walking trails. The Environ-
mental Education center is located at the southern end of the

bay in the Alviso District of San Jose. Its phone number is (408) 262-5513.

San Luis NWR
340 "I" Street
P.O. Box 2176
Los Banos, CA 93635
(209) 826-3508
The refuge has a large wintering population of waterfowl, and a herd of tule elk.

San Pablo Bay NWR
c/o San Francisco Bay NWR Complex
P.O. Box 524
Newark, CA 94560-0524
(510) 792-0222
Located at the northern edge of San Pablo Bay between Vallejo and the Petaluma River, this is the primary wintering area for Pacific Flyway canvasback ducks. Accessible only by foot over a 4-mile trail.

Sutter NWR
c/o Sacramento NWR Complex
Route 1, Box 311
Willows, CA 95988
(916) 934-2801
Peak waterfowl viewing times are in February and March.

Tule Lake NWR
c/o Klamath Basin NWR Complex
Route 1, Box 74
Tulelake, CA 96134
(916) 667-2231
Bald eagles and a million waterfowl in winter, and large summer population of herons, egrets, grebes, terns and gulls are the major attractions at this refuge.

STATE AGENCIES

California Department of Parks and Recreation
P.O. Box 94286
Sacramento, CA 94296
(916) 653-6995
There are 275 state park units in California, and it would take a book to discuss them all. Below are the major units in northern California, with their phone numbers. For more complete information contact the state headquarters. The parks department publishes a small booklet, *California Escapes*, each year that gives a short description of all the state parks and the activities that occur in them.

Region 1—North Coast
Admiral William Standley SRA—(707) 247-3318
A small redwood grove about 15 miles west of U.S. 101 near Laytonville.

Anderson Marsh State Historic Park—(707) 994-0688
Good birdwatching in this park rich in archaeological history.

Annadel SP—(707) 539-3911
A large wilderness park on the outskirts of Santa Rosa with deer and feral hogs. Plenty of hiking trails and wildflowers in the spring.

Armstrong Redwoods State Reserve and Austin Creek SRA—(707) 869-2015
These two units adjoin each other near the Russian River and visitors can enjoy both large groves of redwoods and oak-covered hills.

Azalea State Reserve—(707) 677-3570
A small reserve north of Eureka where wild azaleas are featured each spring.

Bothe-Napa Valley SP—(707) 942-4575
Redwoods, waterfalls and year-round streams are the attractions here.

Del Norte Coast SP—(707) 445-6547
Redwoods reach to the Pacific shoreline in this park just south of Crescent City.

Greenwood Creek State Beach—(707) 937-5804
Seastacks and coastal bluffs rise above the beach here, and the bluffs are a good spot to watch for migrating whales or winter storms. The park is located in the town of Elk along CA 1.

Grizzly Creek Redwoods SP—(707) 777-3683
One of the least-visited redwood parks in the state, Grizzly Creek is located about 17 miles east of U.S. 101.

Hendy Woods SP—(707) 937-5804
Located in Anderson Valley, this park includes groves of huge redwoods and the Navarro River.

Humboldt Lagoons SP/Harry A. Merlo SRA—(707) 488-2041
Lagoons that overflow their sand dams and long beaches where driftwood collects after heavy winter storms are the attractions here.

Humboldt Redwoods SP—(707) 946-2409
The Avenue of the Giants bisects this large park south of Eureka.

Jedediah Smith Redwoods SP—(707) 458-3310
This large redwood park is 9 miles east of Crescent City on CA 199.

Jughandle State Reserve—(707) 937-5804
Pygmy forests and rhododendron displays are the feature

attractions at this park. The geological development of marine terraces is very evident here.

Kruse Rhododendron State Reserve—(707) 847-3221
Large thickets of rhododendron bloom here each spring.

Lakes Earl and Talawa SRA—(707) 464-9533
A variety of coastal habitats are found in this park along the coast.

McKerricher SP—(707) 937-5804
Whale-watching, long beaches and winter storms are all of interest here at this park north of Fort Bragg.

Maillard Redwoods State Reserve—(707) 937-5804
This small, 242-acre redwood park is a good place to go for a quiet walk in the redwoods. It is located to the northwest of Cloverdale.

Manchester SP—(707) 937-5804
Tundra swans and sandy beaches can be found at this park in southern Mendocino County.

Mendocino Headlands SP—(707) 937-5804
Whale-watching and winter storms are the main attractions in this park.

Montgomery Woods State Reserve—(707) 937-5804
This park west of Ukiah off U.S. 101 has a little-used 2-mile hiking trail where you can walk among the giants.

Patrick's Point SP—(707) 677-3570
This park along U.S. 101 north of Trinidad has miles of beaches, tidepools and good wildflowers, as well as whale-watching from high cliffs.

Prairie Creek Redwoods SP—(707) 488-2171
Roosevelt elk and lush fern are found at this redwood park.

Richardson Grove SP—(707) 247-3318
The South Fork of the Eel River passes through this park along U.S. 101 just south of Garberville.

Robert Louis Stevenson SP—(707) 942-4575
This park north of Calistoga features 4,343-foot Mount St. Helena.

Russian Gulch SP—(707) 937-5804
Waterfalls, hiking trails and the ocean are features of this park just north of Mendocino.

Salt Point SP—(707) 847-3221
Pygmy forests, rhododendron and whale-watching are favorite activities here.

Sinkyone Wilderness SP—(707) 986-7711
Forests, prairies, bluffs and beaches provide habitat for many animals and plants in this large park.

Smithe Redwoods State Reserve—(707) 925-0482
This small grove along U.S. 101 offers waterfalls and the Eel River along with redwoods.

Sonoma Coast State Beach—(707) 875-3483
Whale-watching, seal rookery and plenty of beaches are here.

Standish-Hickey SRA—(707) 925-6482
There are few crowds at this redwood park north of Leggett, even in summer.

Sugarloaf Ridge SP—(707) 833-5712
Over 25 miles of trails lead through fields of wildflowers and to the top of grass-covered ridges in this park near Santa Rosa.

Van Damme SP—(707) 937-5804
Fern canyons and a pygmy forest are attractions here.

Region 2—North Inland
Auburn SRA—(916) 885-4527
The three forks of the American River are the main attractions here.

Benicia SRA—(707) 648-1911
Bird-watching in the marshes draws people to this park.

Burton Creek SP—(916) 525-7232
This park has wildflowers, mountain streams and is not very crowded for being located so close to Lake Tahoe.

Castle Craggs SP—(916) 235-2684
Almost 30 miles of hiking trails lead among granite spires that are a geological wonder in this park off I-5 north of Redding.

Colusa-Sacramento River SRA—(916) 458-4927
Bird-watching and boating on the river are enjoyed at this park near downtown Colusa.

D. L. Bliss SP—(916) 525-7277
This is an extremely crowded park in the summer as people come to enjoy the best beach on Lake Tahoe, but streams and mountain meadows with good wildflowers are just a walk away form the crowds.

Donner Memorial SP—(916) 582-7892
Wildflowers, hummingbirds and good hiking are enjoyed at
this park on the eastern end of Donner Lake.

Emerald Bay SP—(916) 525-7277
This park adjoins D. L. Bliss SP and has trails that lead into
the backcountry of Desolation Valley.

Folsom Lake SRA—(916) 988-0205
Plenty of trails lead to wildflowers and rattlesnakes in this
park near Sacramento.

Grover Hot Springs SP—(916) 694-2248
The hot springs are a favorite at this park in the High Sierra
outside Markleeville.

McArthur-Burney Falls Memorial SP—(916) 335-2777
The 129-foot-high waterfall is the feature of this park outside
Redding.

Plumas-Eureka SP—(916) 836-2380
Beaver are a major attraction in this park north of Donner
Lake.

Sugar Pine Point SP—(916) 525-7982
This is the largest state park in the Lake Tahoe basin, and
wildflowers are a main attraction early in the summer.

Woodson Bridge SRA—(916) 839-2112
While most people who use this park come for the fishing,
others like to look for birds in the fine riparian habitat.

Region 3—Central Coast
Andrew Molera SP—(408) 667-2315
This lightly-used park near Big Sur features trails and good
whale-watching.

Angel Island SP—(415) 435-2131
This park is an island in the middle of San Francisco Bay
where you can hike to the top of Mt. Livermore to get
excellent views of the Golden Gate Bridge and San Francisco.

Año Nuevo State Reserve—(415) 879-2027
Elephants seals are a prime attraction at this coast beach
between Half Moon Bay and Santa Cruz.

Big Basin Redwoods SP—(408) 338-6132
The oldest state park in California, Big Basin has many miles
of trails that lead into thick growths of coast redwoods.

Butano SP—(415) 879-0173
Another good redwood park, Butano lies inland from CA 1
about 5 miles.

Forest of Nisene Marks SP—(408) 335-4598
This is a hikers' park near Santa Cruz with very limited access
except on foot.

Monterey State Beaches—(408) 384-7695
These beaches are for walking and bird-watching.

Mount Tamalpais SP—(415) 388-2070
This is a hiker's paradise with plenty of waterfalls in the
winter.

Olompali State Historic Park—(415) 892-3383
Wildflowers cover the hillsides of this park north of Novato
in the springtime.

Point Lobos State Reserve—(408) 624-4909
Sea otters, whales and monarch butterflies all are attractions
at this park south of Carmel.

Samuel P. Taylor SP—(415) 488-9897
Redwoods, ferns and spawning salmon are all in this park in western Marin County.

Tomales Bay SP—(415) 669-1140
Wildflowers and birds are special attractions in this park along Tomales Bay in Point Reyes National Seashore.

Region 3—Central Inland
Bodie State Historic Park—(619) 647-6445
Sage grouse can be seen in strut on the deserted streets of this ghost town off U.S. 395 south of Bridgeport.

Brannan Island SRA—(916) 777-6671
Fishing, boating and birding are all good at this delta park.

Calaveras Big Trees SP—(209) 795-2334
Large groves of giant sequoias are protected in this park east of Stockton in the Sierra foothills.

Caswell Memorial SP—(209) 599-3810
Good wildlife viewing is found among the riparian growth in this park off CA 99 south of Manteca.

George J. Hatfield SRA—(209) 632-1852
This park sits near the confluence of the Merced and San Joaquin rivers, where bird-watching is excellent much of the year.

McConnell SRA—(209) 394-7755
The Merced moves slowly through this recreation area east of Turlock, and wildlife-watching is good. Salmon even come by on their way to spawning grounds farther up-stream.

Millerton Lake SRA—(209) 822-2225
Bald eagles and wading birds like this lake east of Fresno, as do plenty of waterfowl.

Mono Lake Tufa State Reserve—(619) 647-6331
California gulls, phalaropes and grebes all come to this part of the lake to feed on brine shrimp during the spring and summer.

Mount Diablo SP—(415) 837-2525
More than 40,000 square miles of California are visible from this peak east of San Francisco on a clear day. The park also has some of the best wildflower displays in the state.

California Department of Fish and Game
1416 Ninth Street
Sacramento, CA 95814
(916) 653-7664
The department administers about two dozen wildlife areas in Northern California, including Ash Creek, Lake Earl and Grizzly Island, which are discussed in the text. For more information about the wildlife areas contact the department, or the regional office where you wish to visit.

Region 1
601 Locust
Redding, CA 96001
(916) 225-2300

Region 2
1701 Nimbus Road
Rancho Cordova, CA 95670
(916) 355-0978

Region 3
7329 Silverado Trail
Yountville, CA 94599
(707) 944-5500

Region 4
1234 East Shaw Avenue
Fresno, CA 93710
(209) 222-3761

REGIONAL AGENCIES

Most counties in northern California have good park districts
that have many developed parks for picnicking, tennis and
other sports activities. There are also several regional park
districts in California that administer regional parks with
large wilderness areas where you may see spectacular
natural events each year. These include:

East Bay Regional Park District
1150 Skyline Boulevard
Oakland, CA 94619
(510) 531-9300
This district administers over fifty park units in Alameda and
Contra Costa counties, many of which have large wilderness
areas, and provides excellent brochures on the individual units.

Midpeninsula Regional Open Space District
Old Mill Office Center
Building C, Suite 135
201 San Antonio Circle
Mountain View, CA 94040
(415) 949-5500
This district administers several dozen park and open space
units in San Mateo and Santa Clara counties on the San

Francisco Peninsula. Most of the open space units are only marginally developed and are primarily used by hikers and naturalists.

Sacramento County Department of Parks and Recreation
3711 Branch Center Road
Sacramento, CA 95827
(916) 366-2066
The American River Parkway is the showcase for this district.

Solano County Farmlands and Open Space Foundation
P.O. Box 115
Fairfield, CA 94533
(707) 428-7580
Rush Ranch along Suisun Marsh, which is an excellent bird-watching area, is a prime example of this foundation's attempt to combine farming and open space.

PRIVATE AGENCIES

California Native Plant Society
909 12th Street, Suite 116
Sacramento, CA 95814
(916) 447-2677

Mono Lake Committee
P.O. Box 29
Lee Vining, CA 93541
(619) 647-6595

National Audubon Society
Western Regional Office
555 Audubon Place
Sacramento, CA 95825
(916) 481-5332
This office can help you get in contact with your local
Audubon Society chapter as well as your local Christmas
Bird Count coordinator.

The northern California Rare Bird Alert is operated by
the Audubon Society and you can call (510) 528-0288 to
report observations or (510) 524-5592 to hear daily sightings.

The Nature Conservancy California Field and Regional Office
785 Market Street, 3rd Floor
San Francisco, CA 94103
(415) 777-0487
TNC administers, or jointly administers, a dozen preserves in
Northern California where rare and endangered wildlife is
protected from the encroachment of civilization. These
include Elkhorn Slough, Ring Mountain, Jepson Prairie,
McCloud Preserve, Vina Plains and Consumnes River Preserve mentioned in this text. As noted throughout the entries
you should always contact the regional office of TNC before
attempting to enter any preserve.

TNC and Chronicle Books have published *California
Wild Lands* by Dwight Holing, a guide to all Conservancy
preserves in California.

Sierra Club
730 Polk Street
San Francisco, CA 94109
(415) 776-2211
The Sierra Club and its local chapters frequently lead outings
to seasonal natural events. You can obtain information
about local chapters by calling or writing the above.

EDUCATIONAL ACTIVITIES
AND NATURE CENTERS

These educational program, nature centers and science museums frequently offer educational trips to natural events plus seasonal displays of current activities in the natural world. They are administered by national, state, local and private organizations.

Audubon Canyon Ranch
P.O. Box 577
4900 Highway 1
Stinson Beach, CA 94970
(415) 868-9244

Bay Area Mountainwatch
P.O. Box AO
Brisbane, CA 94005
(415) 524-5609

California Academy of Sciences
Golden Gate Park
San Francisco, CA 94118
(415) 750-7142

California Marine Mammal Center
Fort Cronkhite
Sausalito, CA 94965
(415) 331-7325

Clem Miller Environmental Education Center
Point Reyes National Seashore
Point Reyes, CA 94956
(415) 663-1200

Coyote Hills Regional Park
8000 Patterson Ranch Road
Fremont, CA 94536
(510) 795-9385

Coyote Point Museum for Environmental Education
Coyote Point
San Mateo, CA 94401
(415) 342-7755

Discovery Museum Learning Center
3615 Auburn Boulevard
Sacramento, CA 95821
(916) 277-6181

Effie Yeaw Nature Center
Ancil Hoffman Park
P.O. Box 579
Carmichael, CA 95609
(916) 489-4918

Environmental Traveling Companions
Fort Mason Center, Building C
San Francisco, CA 94123
(415) 474-7662

Hayward Shoreline Interpretive Center
4901 Breakwater Ave.
Hayward, CA 94545
(510) 881-6751

Lawrence Hall of Science
University of California
Berkeley, CA 94720
(510) 642-5132

The Lindsay Museum
1901 First Avenue
Walnut Creek, CA 94596
(510) 935-1983

Marin Wildlife Center
76 Albert Park
San Rafael, CA 94901
(415) 454-6961

Marine Science Institute
P.O. Box 7142
Redwood City, CA 94063-7142
(415) 364-2760

Naturalist Associates
107 Palm Avenue
Corte Madera, CA 94925
(415) 924-3572

Oceanic Society
Building E, Fort Mason
San Francisco, CA 94123
(415) 441-5970

Palo Alto Baylands
Lucy Evans Interpretive Center
2775 Embarcadero Road
Palo Alto, CA 94303
(415) 329-2506

Point Reyes Field Seminars
Point Reyes National Seashore
Point Reyes Station, CA 94956
(415) 663-1200

Regional Park Botanic Garden
Tilden Regional Park
Berkeley, CA 94708
(510) 841-8732

Richardson Bay Audubon Center and Sanctuary
376 Greenwood Cove Drive
Tiburon, CA 94920
(415) 388-2524

Shearwater Journeys
P.O. Box 1445
Soquel, CA 95073
(408) 688-1990

Sulphur Creek Nature Center
1801 D Street
Hayward, CA 94541
(510) 881-6747

Terwilliger Nature Education Center
50 El Camino Dr., 5 Gamma Building
Corte Madera, CA 94925
(415) 927-1670

Whale Center
3929 Piedmont Avenue
Oakland, CA 94611
(510) 654-6621

Wildlands Studies
3 Mosswood Circle
Cazadero, CA 95421
(707) 632-5665

SELECTED BIBLIOGRAPHY

Many of the agencies listed above publish free material for those interested in natural events. You can contact the various federal and state agencies asking for a bibliography of their material and then order those pamphlets and tracts that provide information you need for planning your natural outings.

Several publishers have extensive natural history lists that include a number of books on California. The foremost of these publishers is the University of California Press. Their list of California Natural History Guides numbers at least three dozen, and most of these have extensive information on Northern California. These guides are available at local bookstores that carry a good natural history selection, but you can also order them directly from the press at University of California Press, Berkeley, CA 94720; (510) 642-4247 or (800) 777-4726.

Wilderness Press is another publisher with an extensive list of natural history materials covering Northern California. They also have a number of hiking guides to the region. Their books are also found in most local bookstores in California, but are not as well distributed out of state. You can order directly from them at Wilderness Press, 2440M Bancroft Way, Berkeley, CA 94704; (510) 843-8080.

Mountaineer Books, which publishes a wide-ranging series of outdoor and hiking books, have recently begun to publish more hiking books on California. These include my three books in the Best Hikes With Children series. These are *Best Hikes With Children—San Francisco's North Bay*, *Best Hikes With Children—San Francisco's South Bay*, and *Best Hikes With Children Around Sacramento*. In all of these I have included many hikes into natural areas where seasonal events are spectacular. Mountaineer Books are well distributed in bookstores, or you can order from them at Mountaineer Books, 1011 SW Klickitat Way, Suite 107, Seattle, WA 98134; (206) 223-6303.

Other books of interest include:

Arnot, Phil and Elvira Monroe. *Exploring Point Reyes*. San Carlos, CA: Wide World Publishing/Tetra, 1989.

Arora, David. *All That the Rain Promises, and More ... A Hip Pocket Guide to Western Mushrooms*. Berkeley, CA: Ten Speed Press, 1991.

Becking, Rudolf W. *Pocket Flora of the Redwood Forest*. Covelo, CA: Island Press, 1982.

Clark, Jeanne L. *California Wildlife Viewing Guide*. Helena, MT: Falcon Press, 1992.

Hodgson, Michael. *America's Secret Recreation Areas*. San Francisco, CA: Foghorn Press, 1993.

Holing, Dwight. *California Wild Lands—A Guide to The Nature Conservancy Preserves*. San Francisco, CA: Chronicle Books, 1988.

Lyons, Kathleen and Mary Beth Cooney-Lazaneo. *Plants of the Coast Redwood Region*. Boulder Creek, CA: Looking Press, 1988.

Mandel, Stephanie. *The American River: North, Middle, & South Forks*. Auburn, CA: The Wilderness Conservancy, 1989.

Perry, John and Jane Greverus. *The Sierra Club Guide to the Natural Areas of California*. San Francisco, CA: Sierra Club Books, 1983.

Riley, Laura and William. *Guide to the National Wildlife Refuges.* New York, NY: Collier Books, 1992.

Stienstra, Tom. *Great Outdoor Getaways to the Bay Area and Beyond.* San Francisco, CA: Foghorn Press, 1993.

————. *The Complete Guide to California Camping.* San Francisco, CA: Foghorn Press, 1993.

Storer, Tracy and Robert Usinger. *Sierra Nevada Natural History.* Berkeley, CA: University of California Press, 1966.

Westrich, Lolo and Jim. *Birder's Guide to Northern California.* Houston, TX: Gulf Publishing Company, 1991.

Whitnah, Dorothy. *An Outdoor Guide to the San Francisco Bay Area.* Berkeley, CA: Wilderness Press, 1984.

Whitney, Stephen. *A Sierra Club Naturalist's Guide to the Sierra Nevada.* San Francisco, CA: Sierra Club Books, 1979.

————. *A Sierra Club Naturalist's Guide to the Pacific Northwest.* San Francisco, CA: Sierra Club Books, 1989.

Yeaw, Effie. *The Outdoor World of the Sacramento Region.* Sacramento, CA: The American River Natural History Association, 1993.

INDEX

ABOUT THE AUTHOR

Bill McMillon is a naturalist and writer who has sold over 300 articles to regional and national magazines and newpapers. He lives in Sebastopol, California.